WORLD'S GREATEST
STANDARDS

Easy Piano

*52 of the World's Most Popular and
Best Loved Standards*

Selected and Arranged by
DAN FOX

We all know and enjoy songs that we hear every day, but after a few weeks, we sometimes tire of them and move on to new melodies. Standards, however, are something else. These are songs that have been around for years—songs that have been recorded many, many times by a variety of artists and presented in a myriad of settings. This book presents 52 standards in fresh, easy-to-play arrangements.

Included are great show tunes by George and Ira Gershwin, Cole Porter, Rodgers & Hart, Kurt Weill and Lerner & Loewe. There are also timeless movie themes such as *At Last*, *Blues in the Night*, *Laura*, *Over the Rainbow*, and *Somewhere My Love*. In addition, this collection also includes some more recent standards like the *Theme from New York, New York*, *The Wind Beneath My Wings* and *Killing Me Softly with His Song*. Jazz players, who always seem to recognize a good tune when they hear one, will enjoy *Star Dust*, *I Can't Get Started*, *As Time Goes By*, *Don't Get Around Much Anymore*, *I Got Rhythm* and *Satin Doll*.

World's Greatest Standards will surely provide hours of enjoyment as you play these fantastic arrangements of some of the best standard songs ever written.

Alfred

ISBN-10: 0-7390-6079-1
ISBN-13: 978-0-7390-6079-7

CONTENTS

This song is prominently featured in the 1942 film classic *Casablanca,* starring Humphrey Bogart and Ingrid Bergman. Written in 1931 by Herman Hupfeld, nothing much happened with the song until 11 years later, when it appeared as the love song that the film's characters asked the nightclub's pianist to play. (This is the origin of the phrase "Play it again, Sam," even though Bogart never says these exact words.)

As Time Goes By

Words and Music by
Herman Hupfeld

Gordon and Warren, a couple of songwriting pros, turned out this fine ballad for the 1942 movie *Orchestra Wives*. Glenn Miller and his orchestra were prominently featured in this surprisingly true-to-life look at the big band era and the women who stood behind the men who made the music. At the 2009 Inaugural Ball, Barack and Michelle Obama danced together—for the first time as President and First Lady—to the music of "At Last," insuring the continued popularity of this great standard.

At Last

Music by Harry Warren
Lyric by Mack Gordon

Actress and singer Vivienne Segal introduced this song in the 1940 Rodgers and Hart musical *Pal Joey*, based on a novel by John O'Hara. In the Broadway show, the thoroughly disreputable antihero, Joey (played by Gene Kelly in the role that made him a star), exploits the women around him, but eventually gets his comeuppance. Frank Sinatra later played Joey in the 1957 film version.

BEWITCHED, BOTHERED AND BEWILDERED

Words by Lorenz Hart
Music by Richard Rodgers

George and Ira Gershwin wrote this gem for their 1930 musical *Girl Crazy*, in which it was performed by Ginger Rogers. It also appeared in the 1992 musical *Crazy for You*, based on the earlier show. "But Not for Me" has been recorded by virtually every important jazz artist including Ella Fitzgerald, John Coltrane and The Modern Jazz Quartet.

BUT NOT FOR ME

Music and Lyrics by
George Gershwin and Ira Gershwin

Originally written for a 1941 film called *Hot Nocturne*, "Blues in the Night" proved to be such an outstanding song that the film's title was changed to the song title. It was nominated for an Academy Award and has been recorded by many great artists including Dinah Shore, Louis Armstrong, Tex Beneke, Bing Crosby and Rosemary Clooney.

BLUES IN THE NIGHT

Words by Johnny Mercer
Music by Harold Arlen

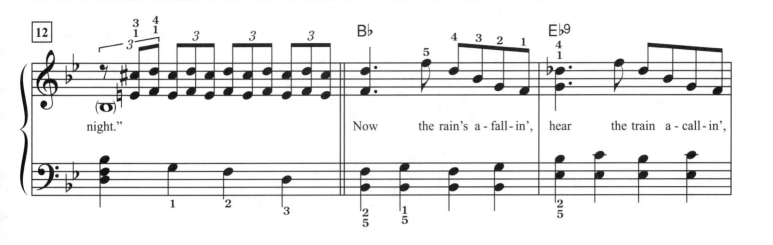

night." Now the rain's a-fall-in', hear the train a-call-in',

whoo-ee._____ (My ma-ma done tol' me.)_____ Hear that lone-some whis-tle

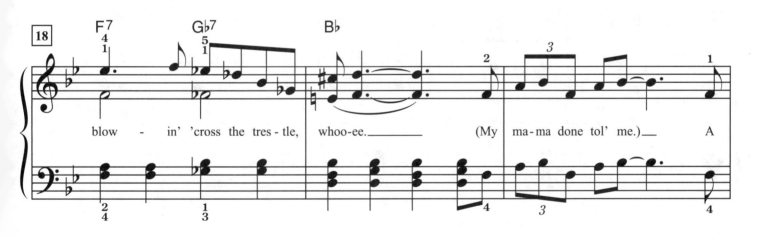

blow - in' 'cross the tres-tle, whoo-ee._____ (My ma-ma done tol' me.)___ A

whoo-ee-duh-whoo-ee,___ ol' click-et-y clack's a - ech-o-in' back the blues_____ in the

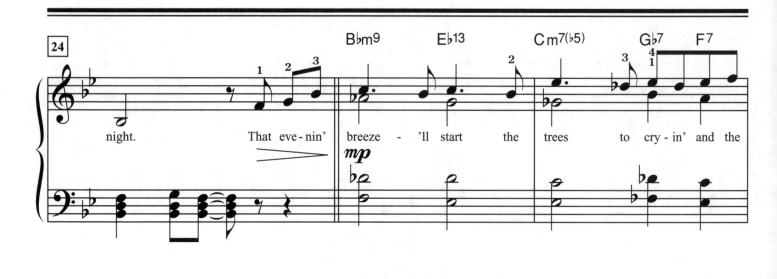

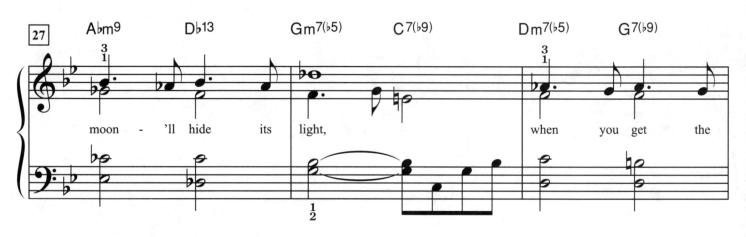

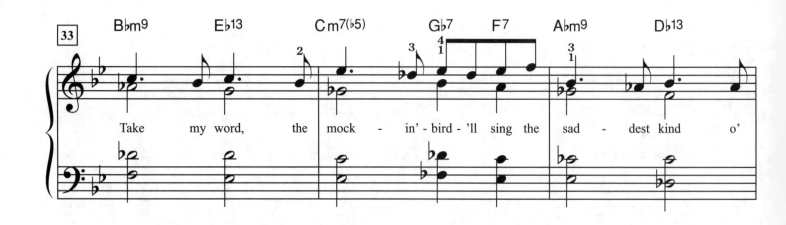

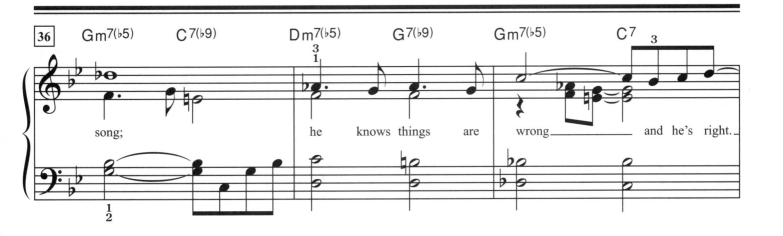

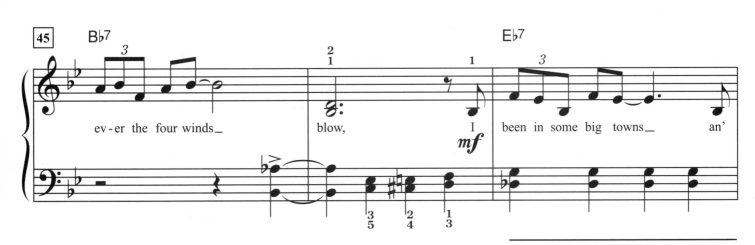

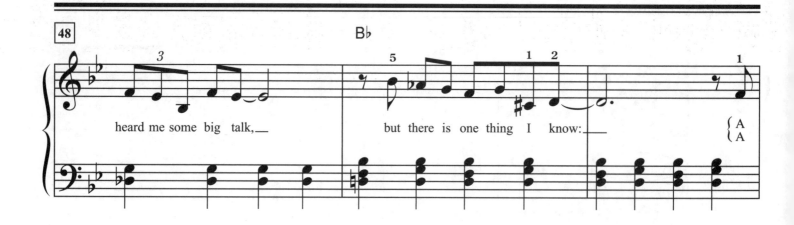

Admired by jazz musicians because of its ingenious chord progression, "Come Rain or Come Shine" was composed by the songwriting team of Johnny Mercer and Harold Arlen for the 1946 film *St. Louis Woman*. It has subsequently been recorded by numerous vocalists and jazz instrumentalists.

COME RAIN OR COME SHINE

Lyrics by Johnny Mercer
Music by Harold Arlen

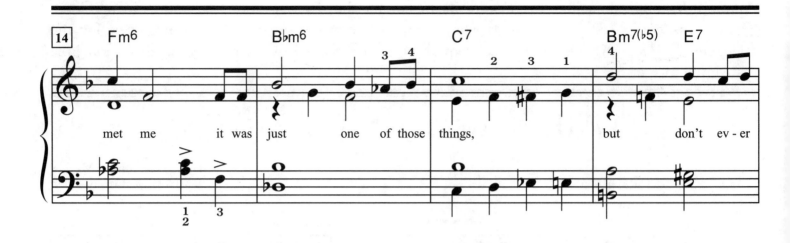

met me it was just one of those things, but don't ev - er

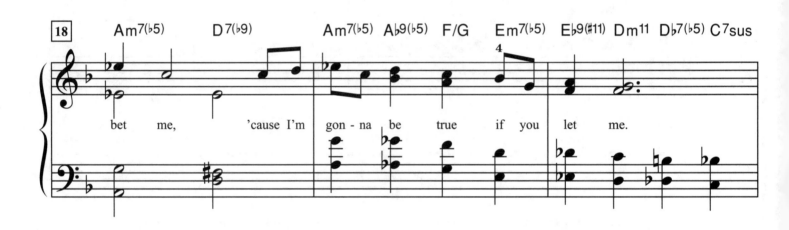

bet me, 'cause I'm gon - na be true if you let me.

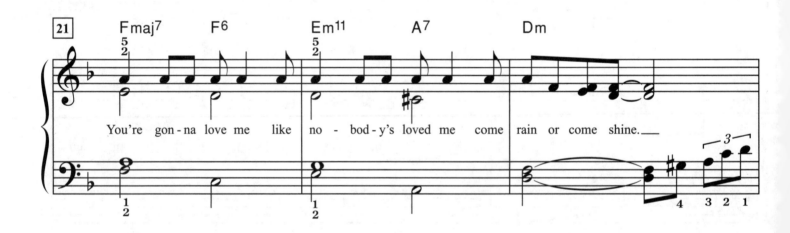

You're gon - na love me like no - bod - y's loved me come rain or come shine.

Hap - py to - geth - er, un - hap - py to - geth - er and

won't it be fine._____ Days may be cloud-y or

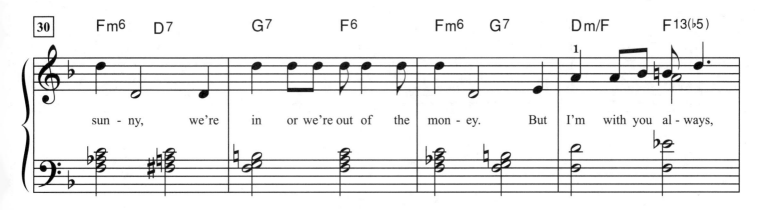

sun - ny, we're in or we're out of the mon - ey. But I'm with you al - ways,

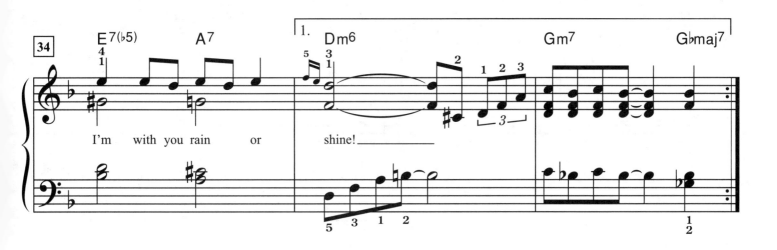

I'm with you rain or shine!_____

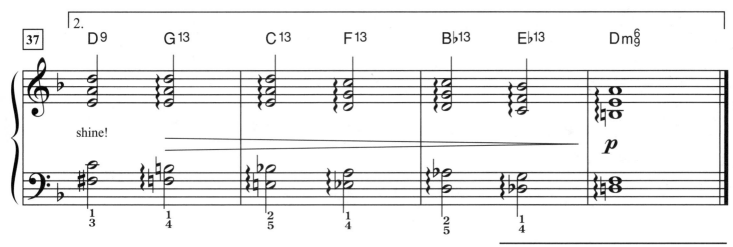

shine!

This classic is one of the many songs by Jimmy Van Heusen and Sammy Cahn that is associated with the greatest of ballad singers, Frank Sinatra. "Come Fly with Me" was the title track for the chart-topping 1958 Sinatra album, and the song became a huge hit.

COME FLY WITH ME

Lyrics by Sammy Cahn
Music by James Van Heusen

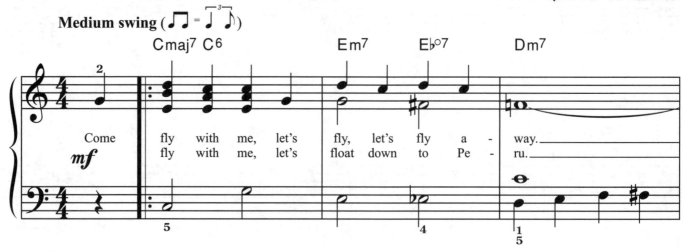

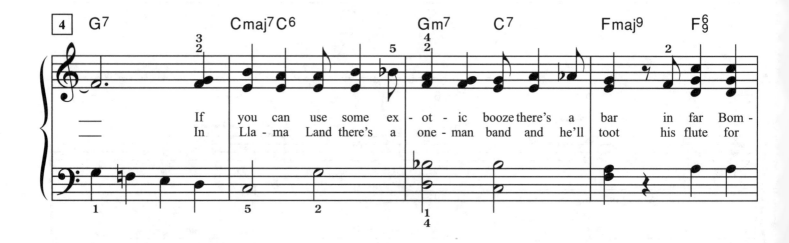

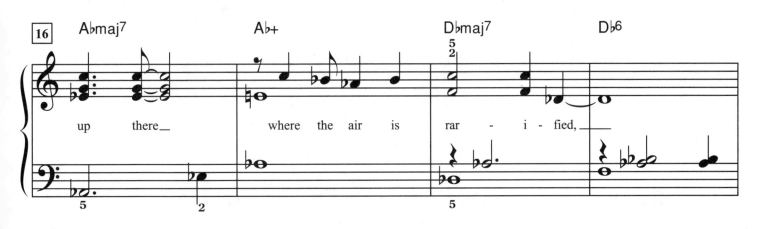

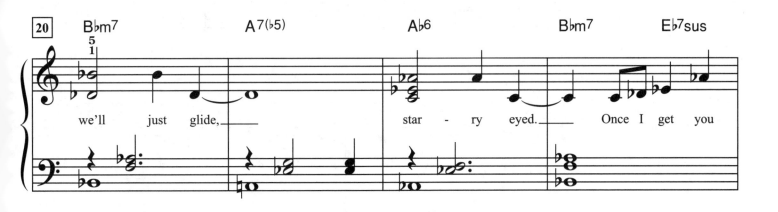

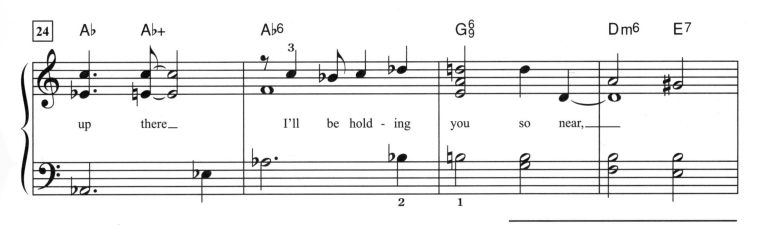

Edward Kennedy "Duke" Ellington was one of the most important figures in the development of jazz in America. Although he studied the piano as a child, he was completely self-taught in the areas of arranging and composition and developed an instantly recognizable style. This classic tune is a fine example of his signature compositional style.

DON'T GET AROUND MUCH ANYMORE

Music by Duke Ellington
Lyrics by Bob Russell

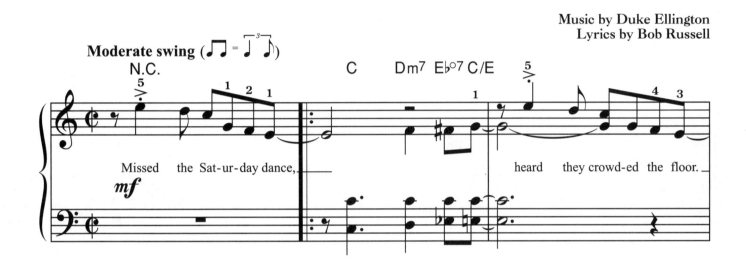

Missed the Sat-ur-day dance, heard they crowd-ed the floor.

Could - n't bear it with - out you;

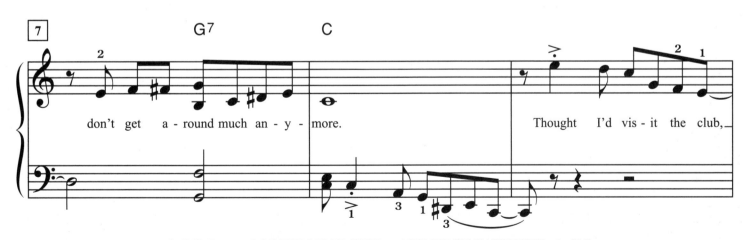

don't get a - round much an - y - more. Thought I'd vis - it the club,

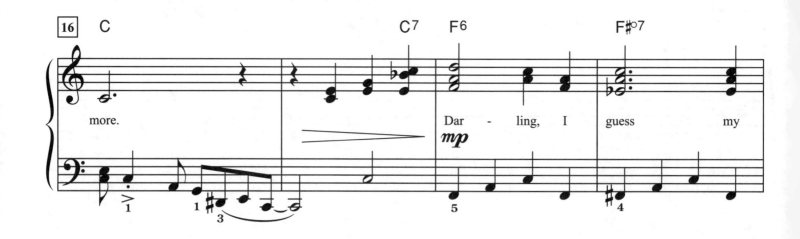

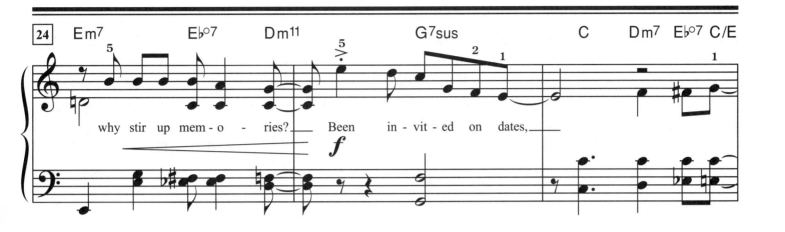

why stir up mem-o-ries? Been in-vit-ed on dates,

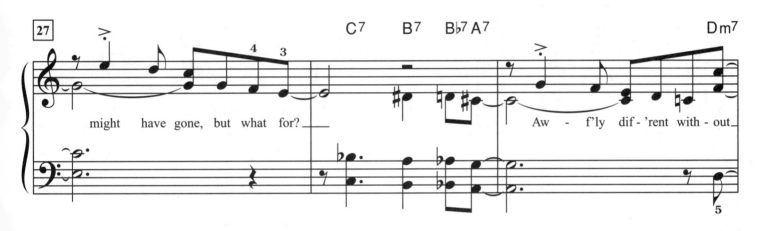

might have gone, but what for? Aw - f'ly dif-'rent with-out

you;_ don't get a-round much an-y-more.

1.

Missed the Sat-ur-day dance,

2.

When George and Ira Gershwin were kids on New York's Lower East Side, their parents bought a piano intended for older brother Ira, but he turned out to be an indifferent student. George, however, would play the instrument whenever he could, and was soon so proficient that he started working for a music publishing firm, promoting songs as a "song plugger." Ira Gershwin started writing witty and sophisticated lyrics, while brother George composed wonderful melodies. The rest, as they say, is history.

EMBRACEABLE YOU

Music and Lyrics by
George Gershwin and Ira Gershwin

One of the most memorable versions of this song was recorded by Frank Sinatra for his 1964 album *It Might as Well Be Swing*. This version was arranged by Quincy Jones, who changed the song's original 3/4 waltz feel to a jazzy 4/4 swing. Those interested in music theory will be intrigued to find that the chord progression is a descending cycle of fifths: A–D–G–C–F–B–E–A.

FLY ME TO THE MOON (IN OTHER WORDS)

Words and Music by Bart Howard

One of George and Ira Gershwin's most enduring standards, "A Foggy Day" was introduced by Fred Astaire in the 1937 film *A Damsel in Distress*. The song has been recorded by many great singers and instrumentalists including Tony Bennett, Frank Sinatra, Ella Fitzgerald, Wynton Marsalis and Sarah Vaughan.

A FOGGY DAY (IN LONDON TOWN)

Music and Lyrics by
George Gershwin and Ira Gershwin

Though far from a household name, J. Fred Coots wrote the music or words for over 700 songs, including many great standards such as "You Go to My Head," "Santa Claus Is Coming to Town," "Love Letters in the Sand," and this song, penned in 1934 and revived by the Nat King Cole Trio in the late 1940s.

For All We Know

Words by Sam M. Lewis
Music by J. Fred Coots

This song was first in the 1941 film *Babes on Broadway*, starring Mickey Rooney and Judy Garland. Its catchy rhythm and interesting chord progression soon made "How About You?" a favorite of jazz musicians everywhere.

How About You?

Music by Burton Lane
Words by Ralph Freed

Joseph Schillinger was a composer and theorist who developed a mathematical way of composing music. In the 1920s, George Gershwin became interested in Schillinger's ideas, especially as they applied to cross-rhythms. This 1924 tune is one result (also see "I Got Rhythm" in this book). The main theme consists of seven eighth notes superimposed on a four-quarter rhythm. Fascinating indeed!

FASCINATING RHYTHM

Music and Lyrics by
George Gershwin and Ira Gershwin

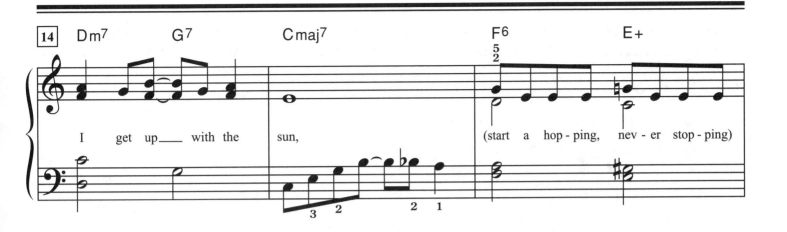

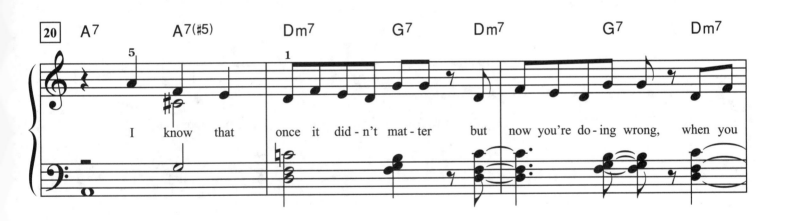

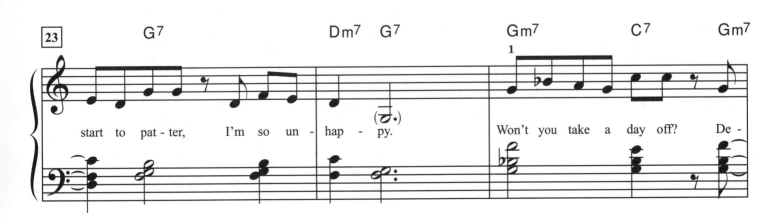

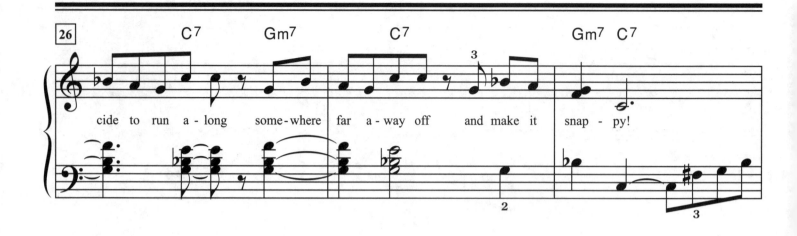

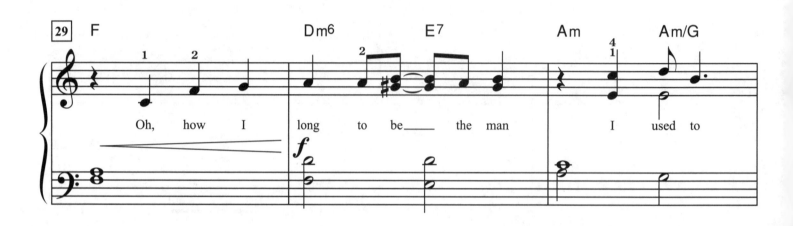

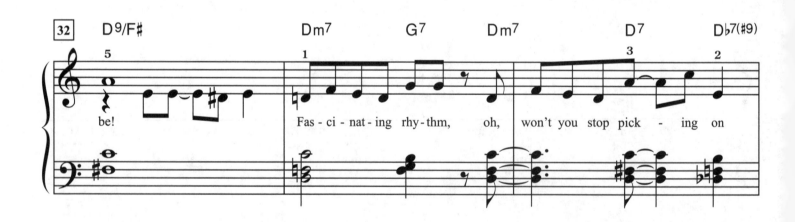

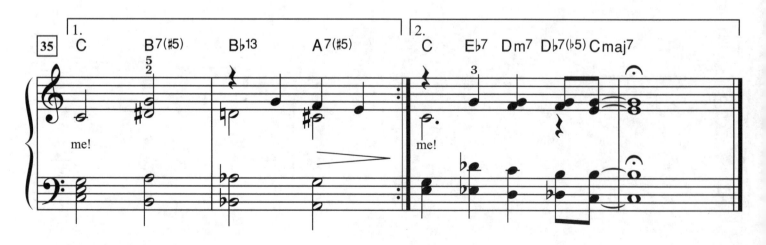

Although originally presented as a love song in a Broadway revue called *Two for the Show* (1940), a hit recording by Benny Goodman at a much faster tempo soon made this song a jazz standard. In 1945, bebop legend Charlie "Yardbird" Parker used its chord progression as the basis for his famous composition "Ornithology." In 1951, Les Paul and Mary Ford used breakthrough technology to create a multi-track rendition, which became the best-known recording of "How High the Moon."

HOW HIGH THE MOON?

Lyrics by Nancy Hamilton
Music by Morgan Lewis

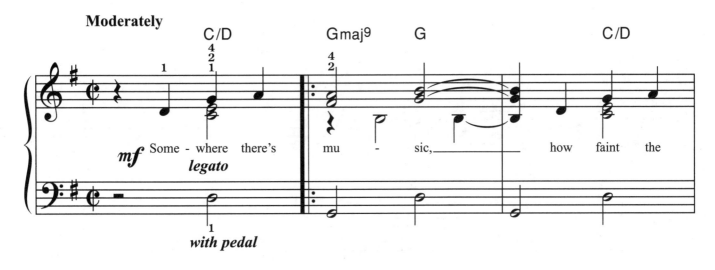

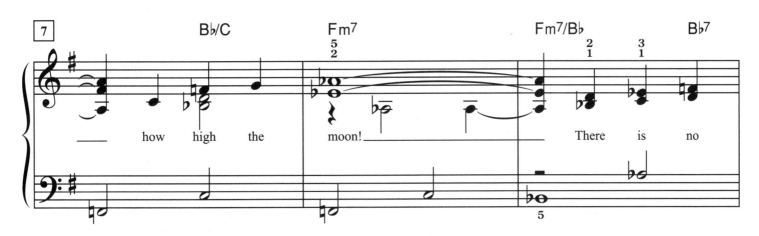

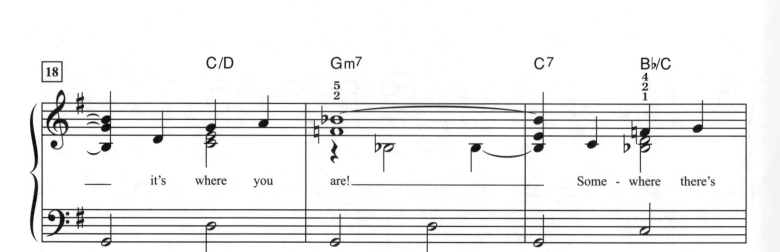

Since brother George was busy composing his opera *Porgy and Bess*, Ira Gershwin teamed up with Vernon Duke to write the score for the musical revue *Ziegfeld Follies of 1936*. The show was not very successful, but this song—forever associated with the trumpet playing and voice of jazz great Bunny Berigan—was a standout.

I Can't Get Started

Words by Ira Gershwin
Music by Vernon Duke

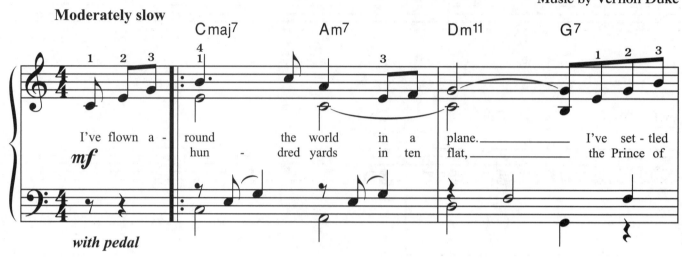

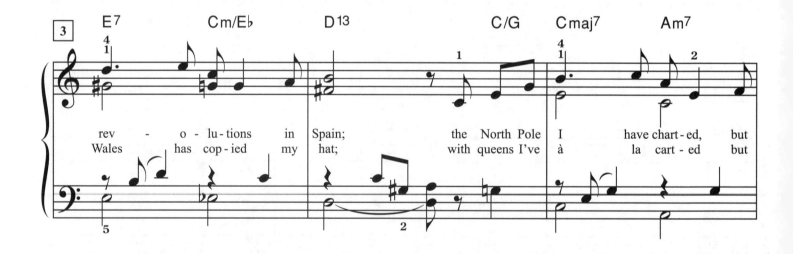

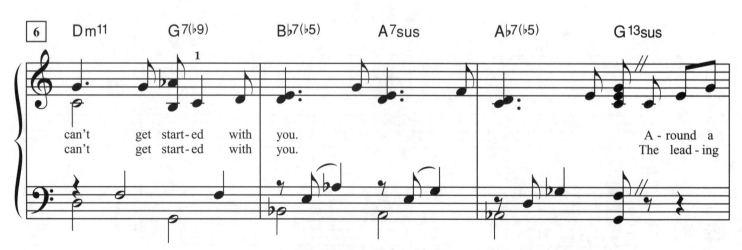

Bandleader Isham Jones led one of the best dance orchestras of the 20s and 30s. Jones was also a talented songwriter with titles such as "I'll See You in My Dreams," "Swingin' Down the Lane," "The One I Love Belongs to Somebody Else," "There Is No Greater Love," and this fine standard. Jones retired in 1938 and his band was taken over by band member and reedman Woody Herman.

It Had to Be You

Words by Gus Kahn
Music by Isham Jones

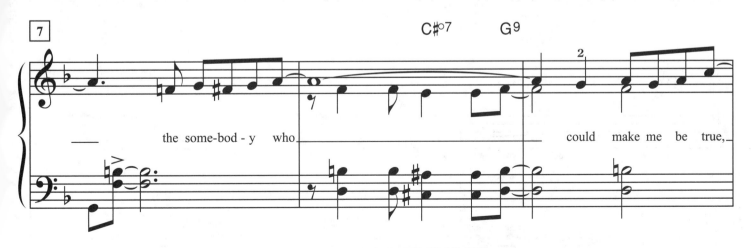

Although the 1920s had not been greatly successful for Cole Porter, the 1930s turned out to be his decade. Hit show followed hit show and it seemed the great songs would never end. In the original 1934 Broadway production of *Anything Goes*, Ethel Merman got to sing five of these hits: *All Through the Night*; *Anything Goes*; *Blow, Gabriel, Blow*; *You're the Top* and this great standard.

I Get a Kick out of You

Words and Music by Cole Porter

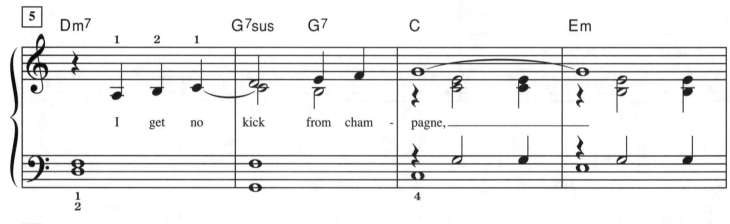

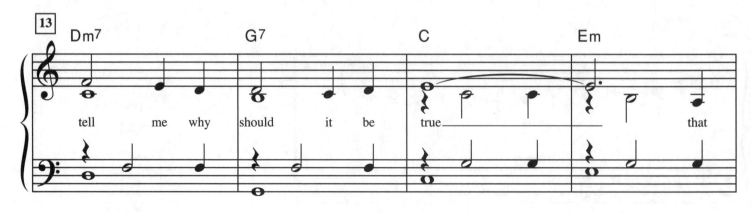

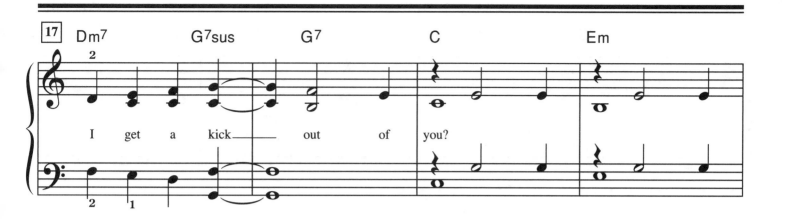

I get a kick _____ out of you?

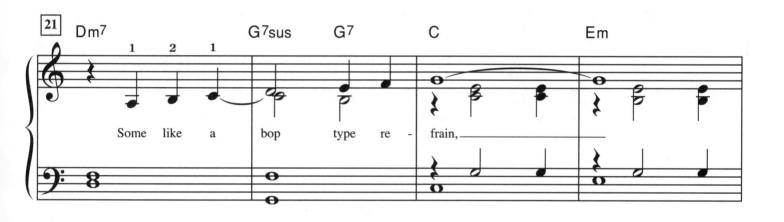

Some like a bop type re - frain, _____

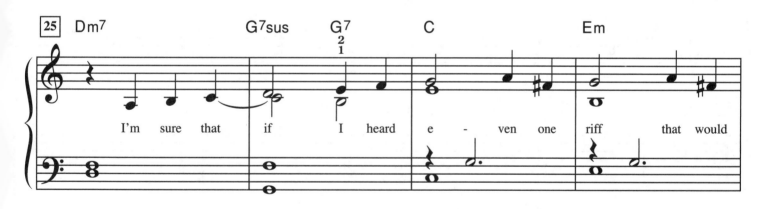

I'm sure that if I heard e - ven one riff that would

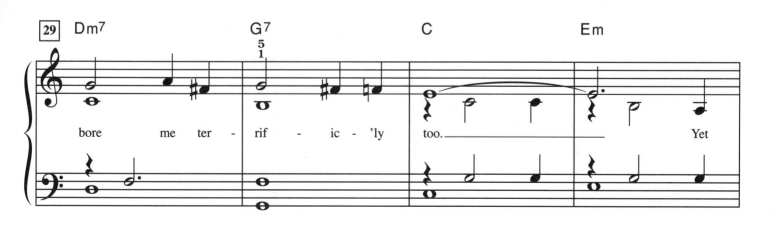

bore me ter - rif - ic - 'ly too. _____ Yet

Ethel Merman's rendition of "I Got Rhythm" in the Gershwin brothers' 1930 musical *Girl Crazy* immediately made the singer a star. The song's chord progression became known to jazz musicians as "the rhythm changes" and serves as the basis for many popular jazz compositions.

I GOT RHYTHM

Music and Lyrics by
George Gershwin and Ira Gershwin

Introduced in 1955 on Frank Sinatra's album of the same name, this song soon became a nightclub favorite. The 1993 film *Sleepless in Seattle,* starring Tom Hanks and Meg Ryan, featured a beautiful Carly Simon rendition of the song, capturing the melancholy of lost love.

IN THE WEE SMALL HOURS OF THE MORNING

Words by Bob Hilliard
Music by Dave Mann

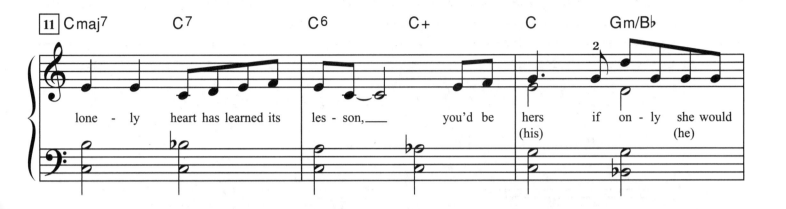

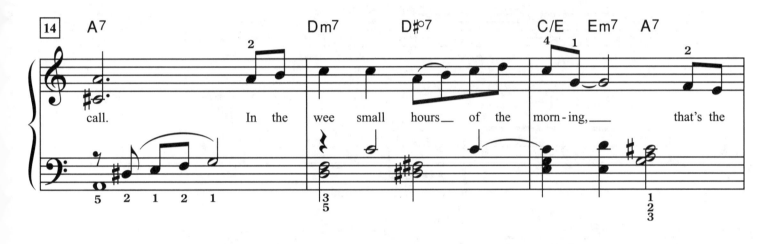

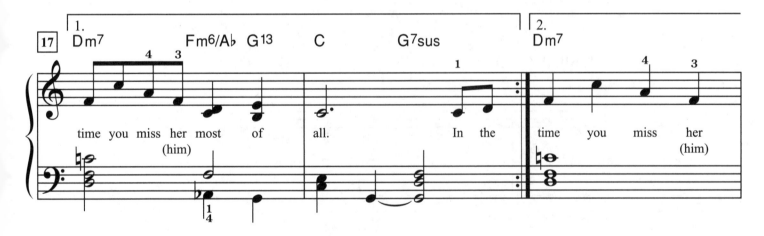

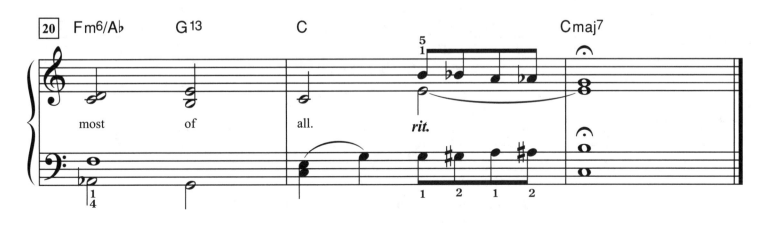

This song is one of many great standards from the pen of Harold Arlen. After a few years as a pianist and vocalist, he began composing songs with lyricists Ted Koehler, Yip Harburg, Johnny Mercer and others. "I've Got the World on a String" was introduced by both Cab Calloway and Bing Crosby, and was recorded in 1952 by Frank Sinatra.

I'VE GOT THE WORLD ON A STRING

Words by Ted Koehler
Music by Harold Arlen

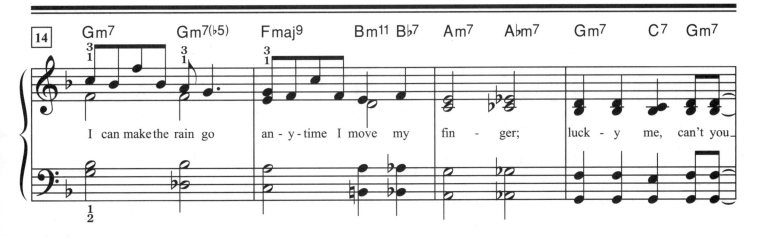

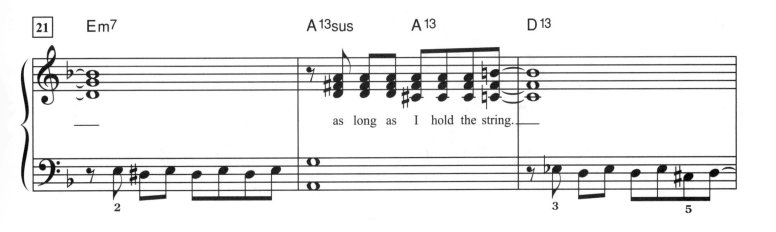

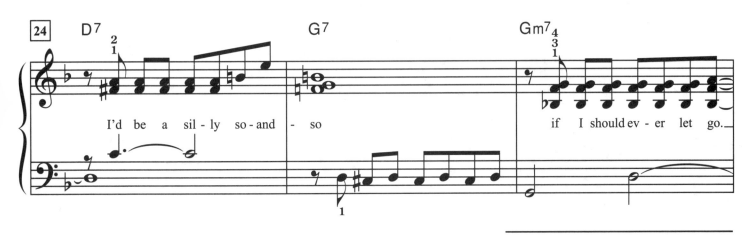

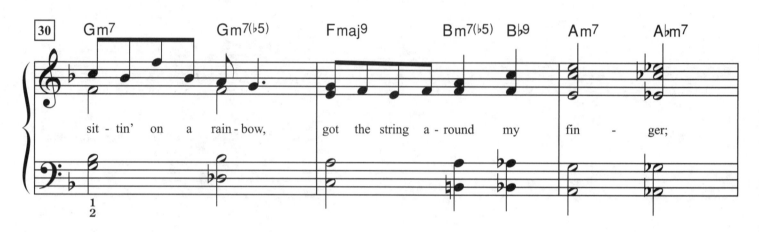

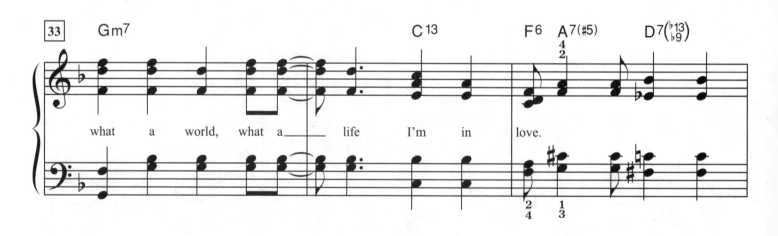

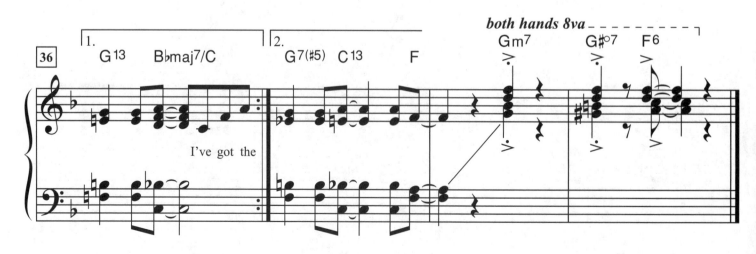

Another gem from the seemingly inexhaustible pen of Cole Porter, this song was featured in the 1936 film *Born to Dance,* which starred the great tap dancer Eleanor Powell, Jimmy Stewart, and Buddy Ebsen. Porter was at the height of his powers and seemed to be the only popular composer of the time who could get away with writing long songs like *Begin the Beguine, Just One of Those Things,* and *I Get a Kick Out of You.*

I'VE GOT YOU UNDER MY SKIN

Words and Music by
Cole Porter

This song, one of Rodgers and Hart's wittiest, was composed for their 1937 Broadway musical *Babes in Arms*. The show also featured the great standards "My Funny Valentine," "The Lady Is a Tramp," "Johnny One Note," and "Where or When." Not too shabby for a show that ran for only 289 performances!

I Wish I Were In Love Again

Words by Lorenz Hart
Music by Richard Rodgers

This is another outstanding song from the prolific pen of Cole Porter. Its ingenious 64-bar structure explores the keys of D minor, B-flat, E-flat and C major, before finally coming to rest in F major. Although written in typical A-A-B-A form, each time the A section appears, it is slightly altered, building to a completely logical climax.

JUST ONE OF THOSE THINGS

Words and Music by Cole Porter

* Small notes are optional.

Originally written by George and Ira Gershwin for the Fred Astaire/Ginger Rogers film *Shall We Dance* (1937), this song has become a favorite of singing duos for its catchy melody and witty lyric. An updated version of *Shall We Dance*, starring Richard Gere, was made in 2004.

LET'S CALL THE WHOLE THING OFF

Music and Lyrics by
George Gershwin and Ira Gershwin

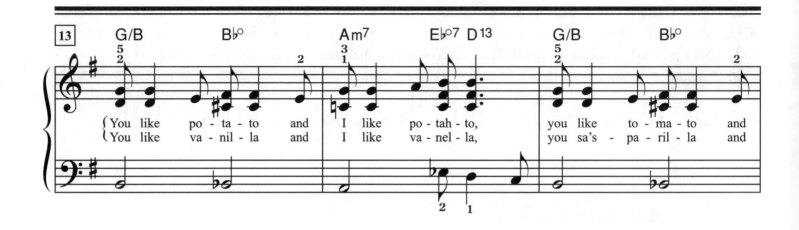

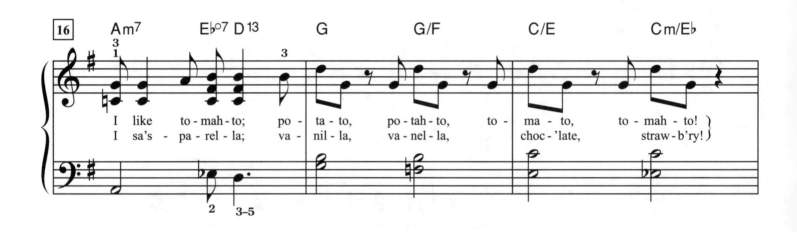

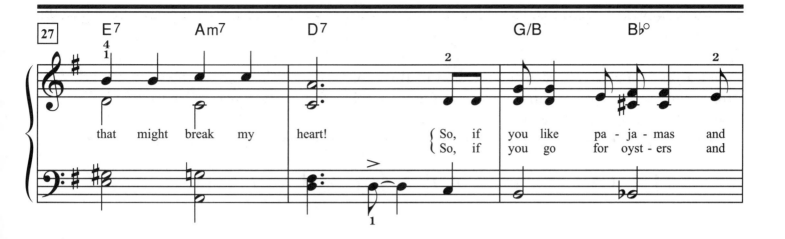

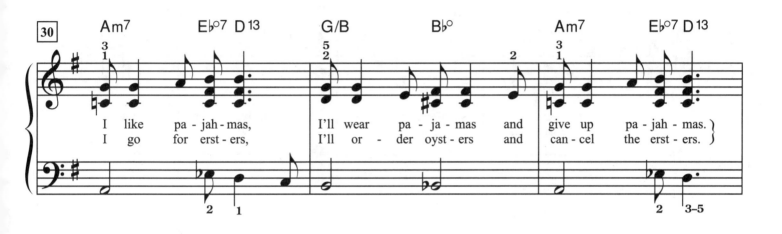

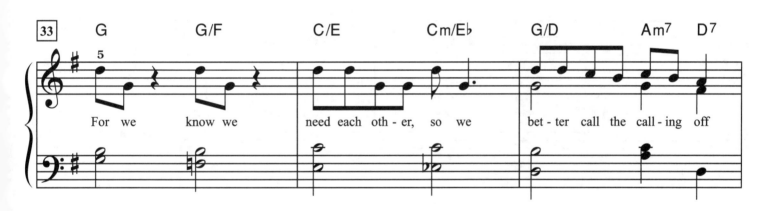

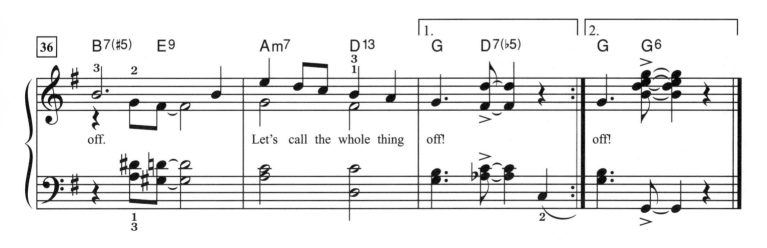

Killing Me Softly with His Song was written overnight by Norman Gimbel and Charles Fox, to quickly complete the first of four albums they produced for singer Lori Lieberman. After the album's release in 1973, American Airlines programmed the record on their inflight entertainment channel, where Roberta Flack heard the song while flying from Chicago to New York. Soon afterwards, Roberta recorded her version of the song, which subsequently became a worldwide No. 1 hit and garnered Grammy awards for Best Record and Best Song. In 1996, The Fugees recorded the song and it became a worldwide hit for the second time.

KILLING ME SOFTLY WITH HIS SONG

Words and Music by
Charles Fox and Norman Gimbel

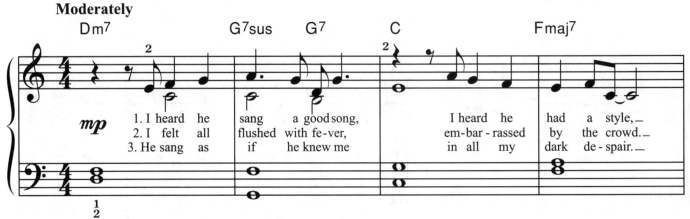

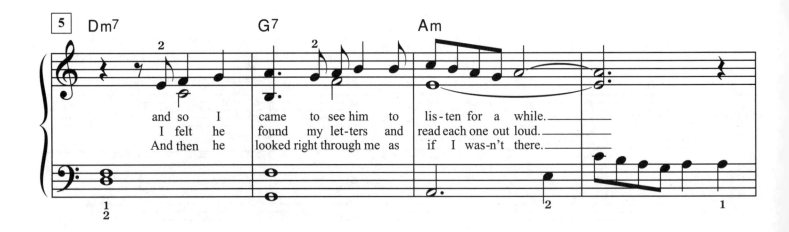

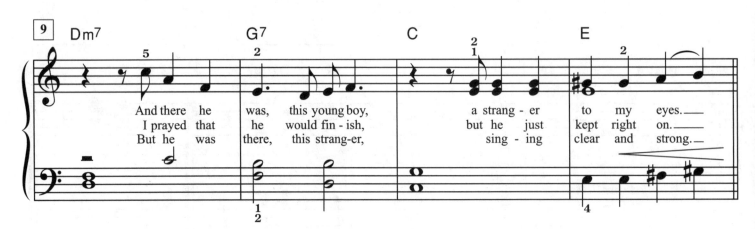

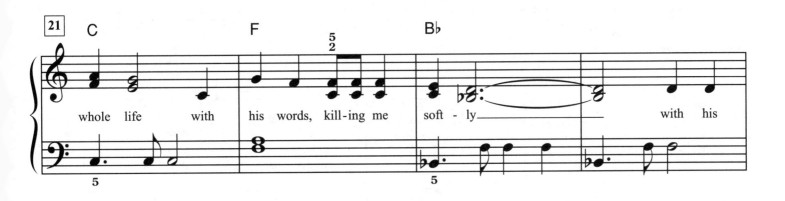

This is another great standard from the score of Rodgers and Hart's 1937 show *Babes in Arms*. Although originally written with the two-beat feel of the "businessman's bounce," jazz players soon started playing it with a swing feel. Outstanding recordings of this classic include those by Frank Sinatra, Shirley Bassey, Ella Fitzgerald and, most famous of all, Lena Horne.

THE LADY IS A TRAMP

Words by Lorenz Hart
Music by Richard Rodgers

The romantic atmosphere of the 1944 classic film *Laura* was provided by Hollywood composer David Raksin, who created a musical score that includes this haunting theme song. Johnny Mercer created some of his finest lyrics for this timeless piece.

Laura

Lyric by Johnny Mercer
Music by David Raksin

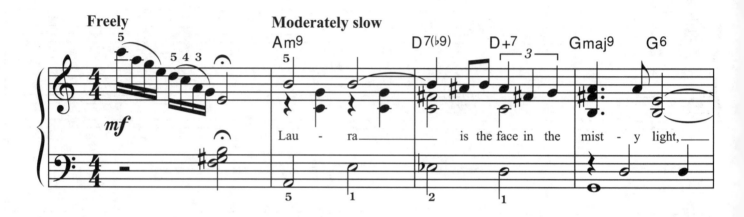

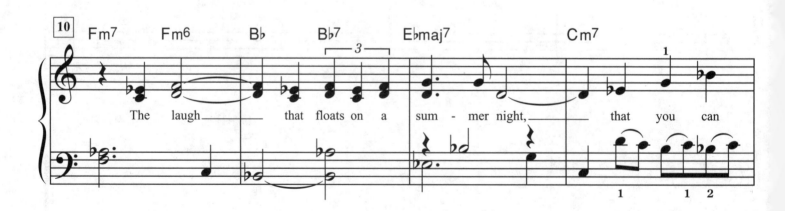

Starting with his first hit in 1919 (*Swanee*), George Gershwin had a seemingly endless series of hit shows, pop tunes and instant classics (*Rhapsody in Blue, An American in Paris, Concerto in F,* the opera *Porgy and Bess* and others). In 1937, Gershwin died of a brain tumor at the age of 38. Luckily for us, he left many sketches for songs, this being one of them, outfitted with a sophisticated lyric by brother Ira several years after George's death.

LOVE IS HERE TO STAY

Lyrics by Ira Gershwin
Music by George Gershwin

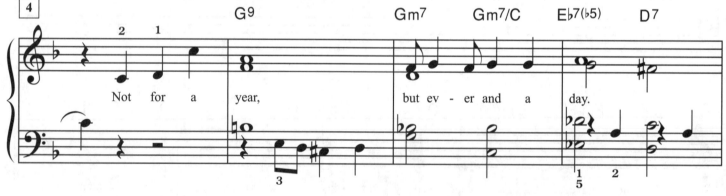

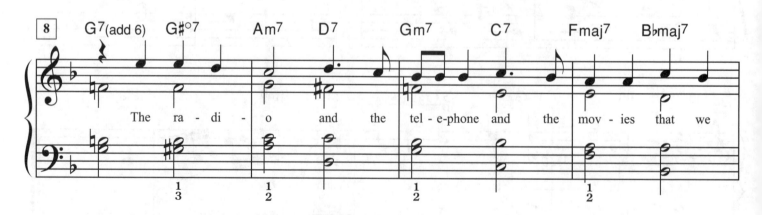

One of the great natural talents in the history of jazz, Erroll Garner started taking piano lessons as a very young child. His teacher thought he was an incredible sight-reader until he figured out that little Erroll was actually memorizing all his assigned pieces after hearing his teacher play them once! Even though Garner never did learn how to read music, he recorded with such jazz stars as Charlie Parker, developed an instantly recognizable hard-swinging style, and wrote the melody to this great standard.

MISTY

Music by Erroll Garner
Words by Johnny Burke

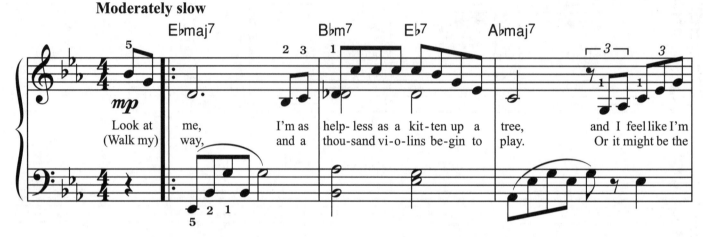

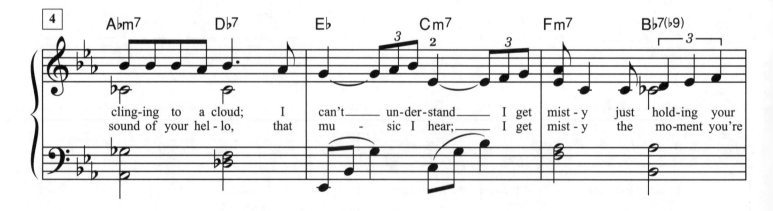

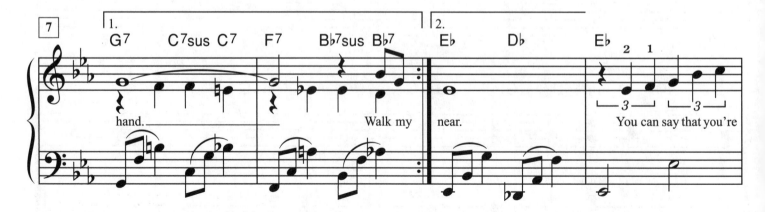

The songwriting team of Rodgers and Hart were already Broadway legends with over a decade's worth of hit shows and memorable standards to their credit when they wrote the music for the 1937 show *Babes in Arms*. The score included *I Wish I Were in Love Again, Where or When,* and this charming and evocative song. The show ran for almost 300 performances. Two years later, Hollywood turned it into a movie starring Mickey Rooney and Judy Garland.

My Funny Valentine

Words by Lorenz Hart
Music by Richard Rodgers

The wonderful singer/comedian Eddie Cantor introduced this song in the 1928 Broadway show *Whoopee!* Prior to that time, "whoopee" simply meant "having a good old time," as in "whooping it up." But Cantor's sly delivery and Gus Kahn's lyrics filled with double-entendres forever changed the meaning of the expression.

MAKIN' WHOOPEE

Lyrics by Gus Kahn
Music by Walter Donaldson

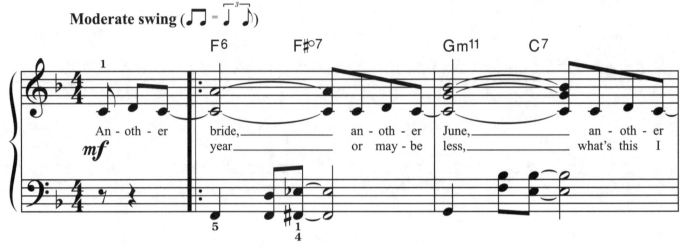

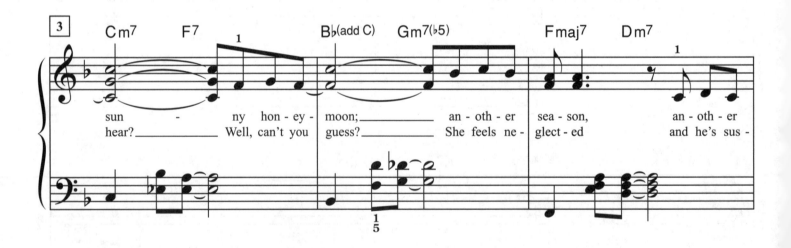

shoes,_____ a lot of rice,_____ the groom is ner - vous,_____ he an - swers
lone_____ most ev - 'ry night._____ He does - n't phone her_____ he does - n't

twice;_____ it's real - ly kill - ing that he's so will - ing to make____
write._____ He says he's "bus - y," but she says, "Is he? He's mak - in'

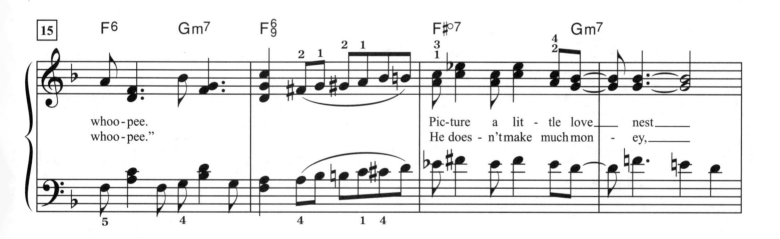

whoo - pee. Pic - ture a lit - tle love____ nest____
whoo - pee." He does - n't make much mon - ey,____

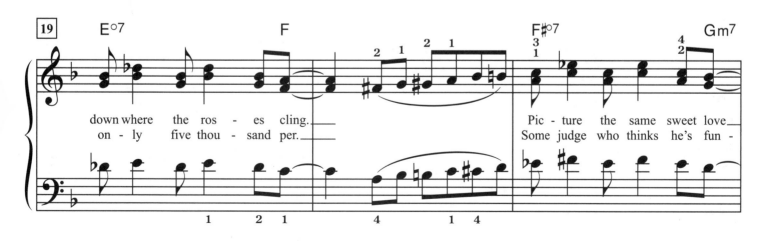

down where the ros - es cling.____ Pic - ture the same sweet love____
on - ly five thou - sand per.____ Some judge who thinks he's fun -

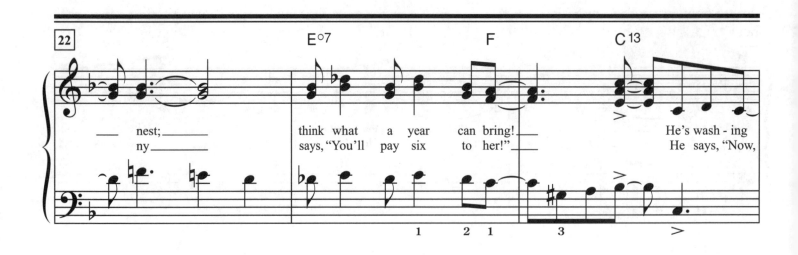

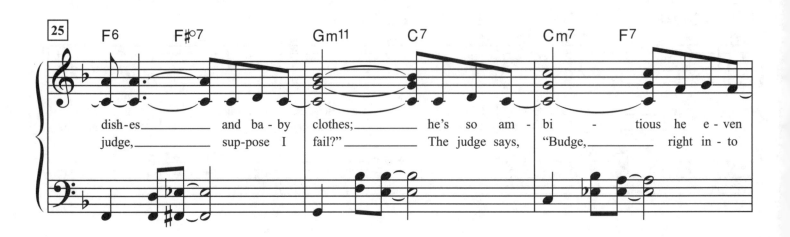

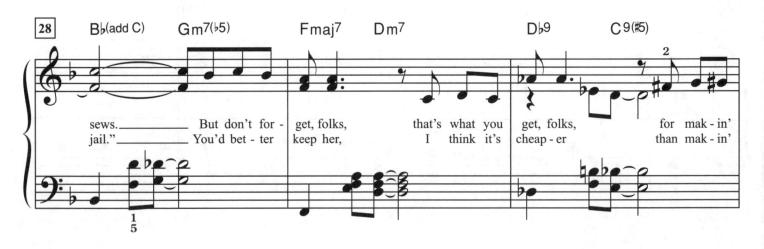

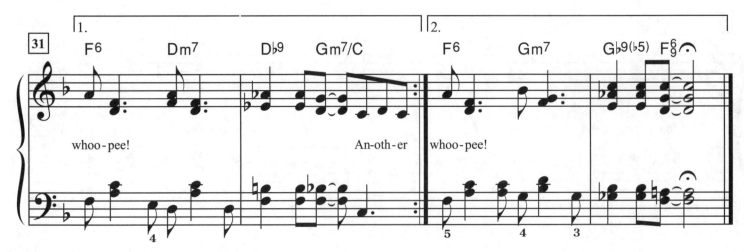

The 1977 movie *New York, New York*, which starred a young Robert DeNiro and Liza Minelli, is best remembered for this theme song. In 1979, Frank Sinatra recorded his famous version of the tune, which became a huge hit.

THEME FROM "NEW YORK, NEW YORK"

Music by John Kander
Words by Fred Ebb

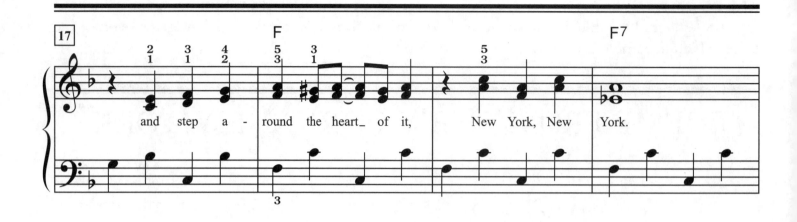

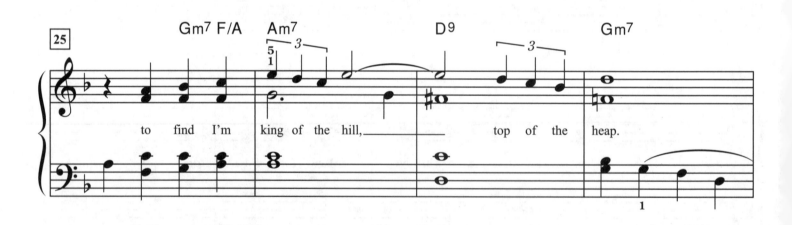

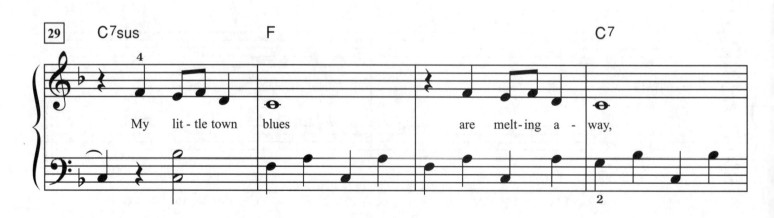

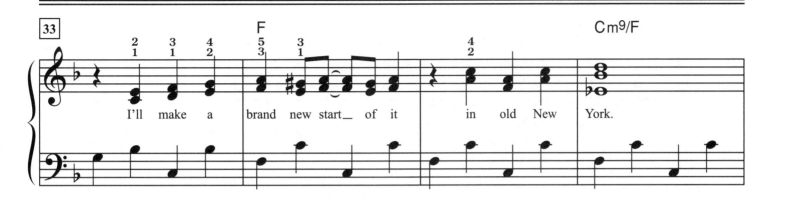

I'll make a brand new start of it in old New York.

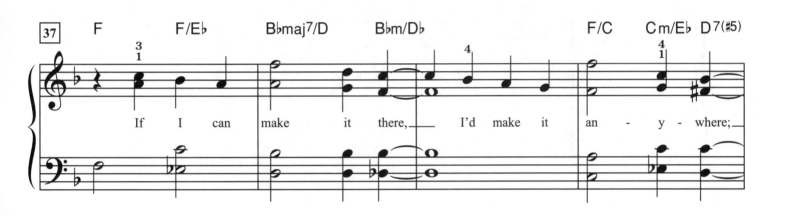

If I can make it there, I'd make it an - y - where;

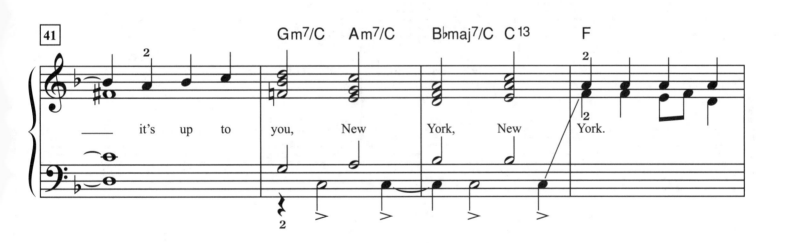

it's up to you, New York, New York.

In the ancient Greek myth, an artist named Pygmalion falls in love with a statue of a beautiful woman that he's sculpted. English playwright George Bernard Shaw transformed this theme into a play, upon which Lerner and Loewe based their highly successful musical, *My Fair Lady* (1956). The show was later made into a movie with Rex Harrison repeating his Broadway role and Audrey Hepburn as the Cockney girl who learns to speak like a lady.

ON THE STREET WHERE YOU LIVE

Words by Alan Jay Lerner
Music by Frederick Loewe

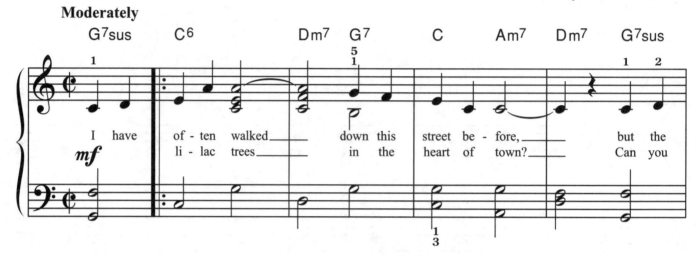

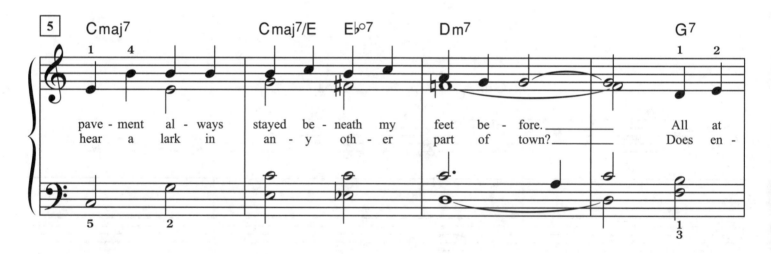

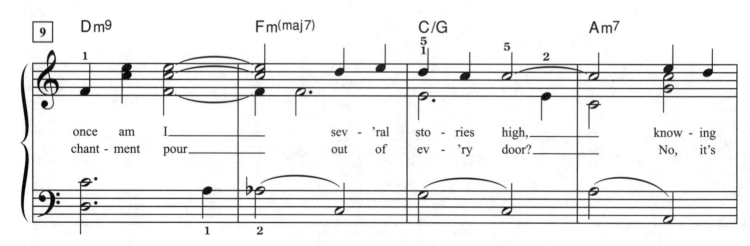

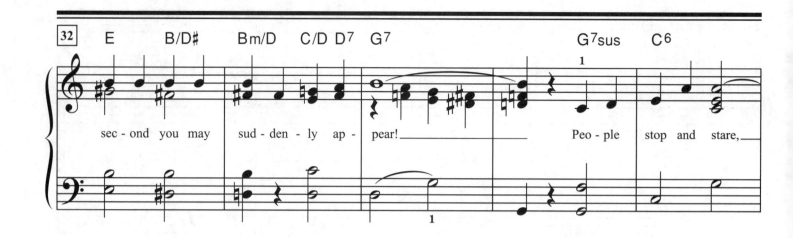

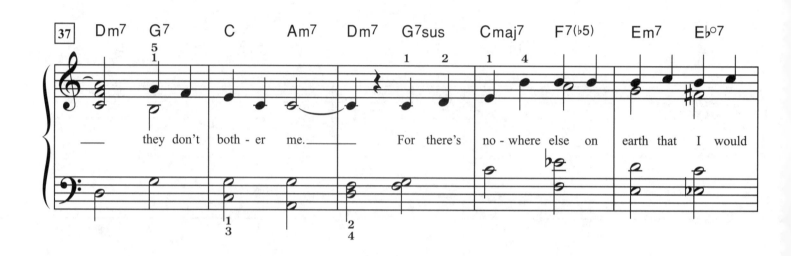

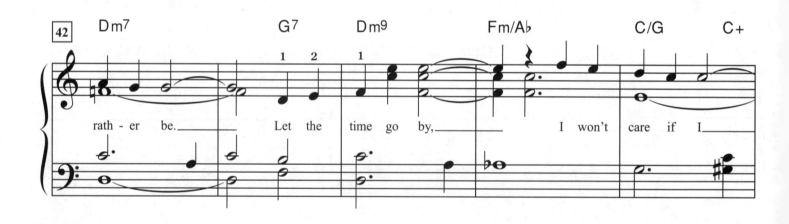

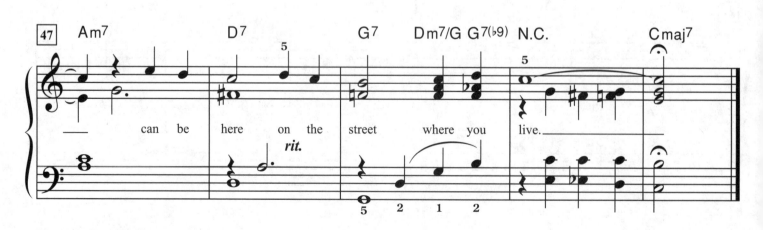

Hollywood executives tried several times to drop this beloved song from the 1939 movie *The Wizard of Oz*, complaining that it slowed the action down. Thankfully this point of view didn't prevail, and Judy Garland's rendition became one of the highlights of the film. The song went on to become her theme song, and was recorded hundreds of times by both popular and jazz artists.

OVER THE RAINBOW

Music by Harold Arlen
Lyric by E. Y. Harburg

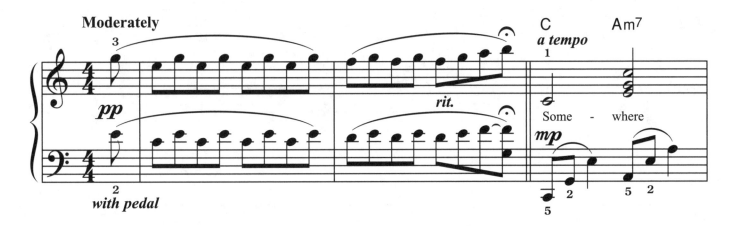

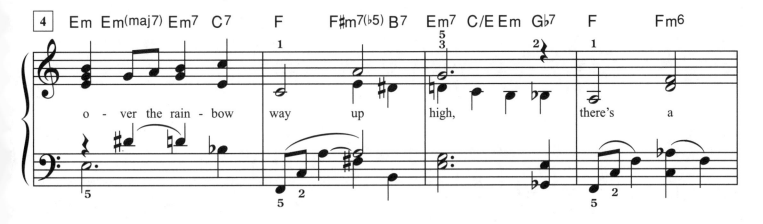

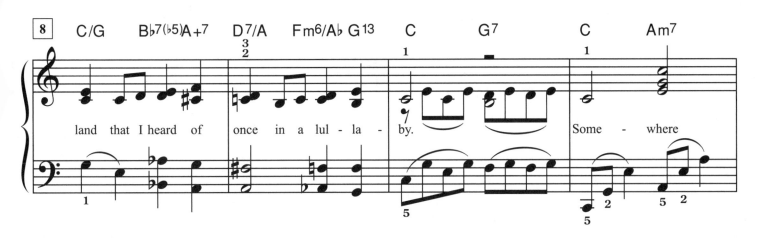

Barbra Streisand was hardly known outside of New York City when, in 1963, she was chosen to star in *Funny Girl*, a Broadway musical about the life of comedienne Fanny Brice. The show became a big hit, due in part to the timeless song People. In 1968, *Funny Girl* was turned into a motion picture, for which Streisand earned an Academy Award for Best Actress.

PEOPLE

Words by Bob Merrill
Music by Jule Styne

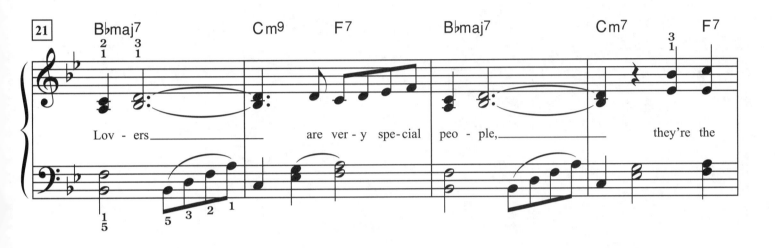

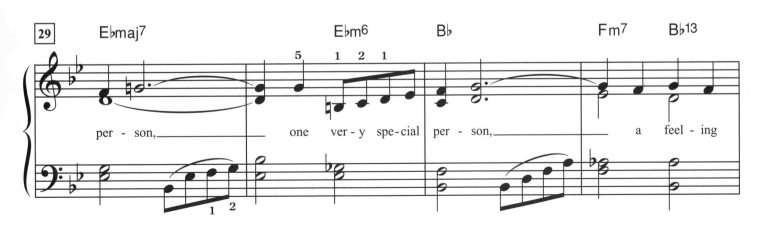

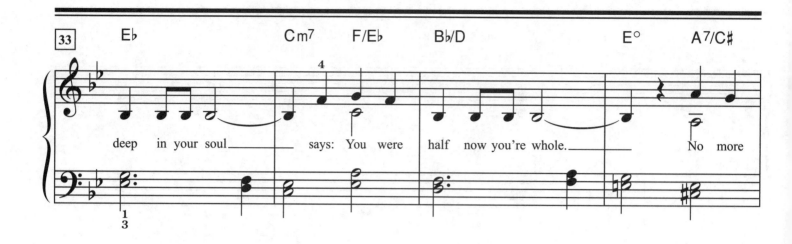

deep in your soul____ says: You were half now you're whole.____ No more

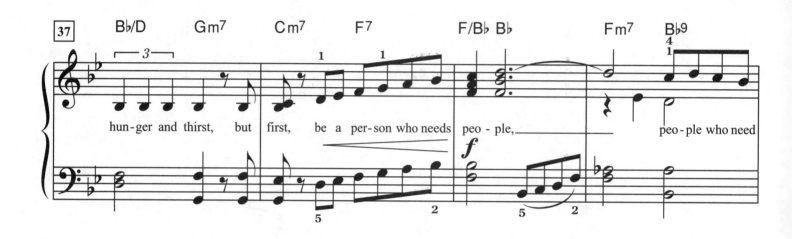

hun-ger and thirst, but first, be a per-son who needs peo - ple,____ peo - ple who need

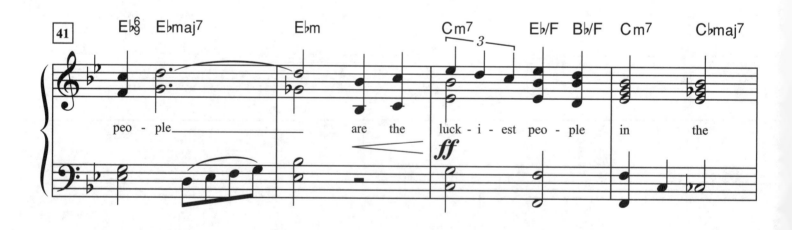

peo - ple____ are the luck-i-est peo - ple in the

1.
world.____

2.
world.

Jazz great Duke Ellington and frequent collaborator Billy Strayhorn wrote this standard as an instrumental in 1953. By 1958, jazz musicians were playing the song so often that Duke asked Johnny Mercer to add some lyrics. The result is a witty, unforgettable classic.

SATIN DOLL

Words and Music by
Johnny Mercer, Duke Ellington and Billy Strayhorn

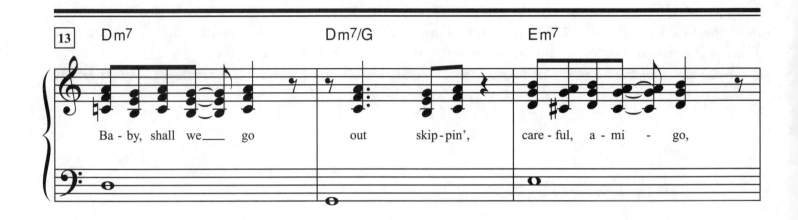

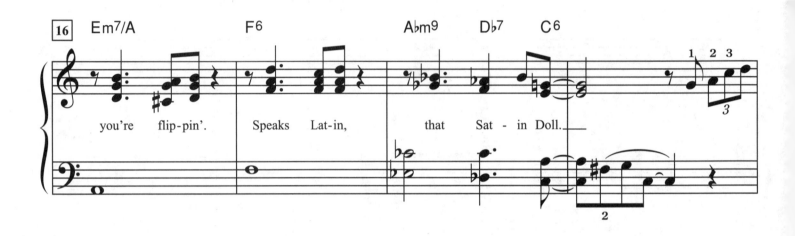

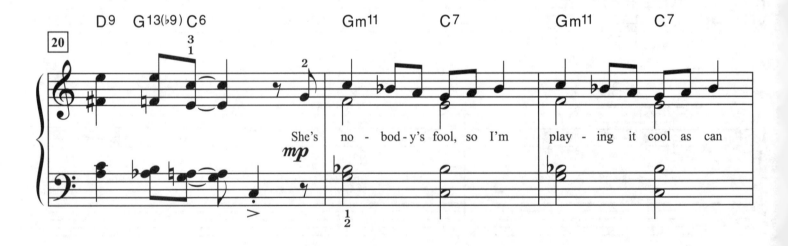

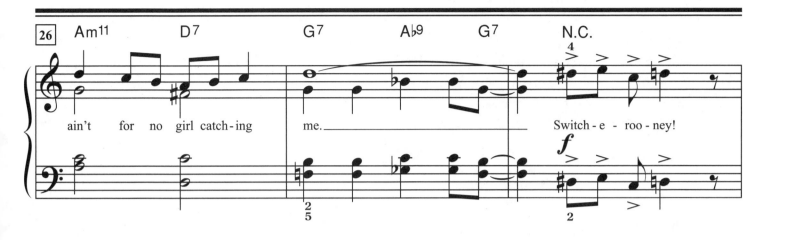

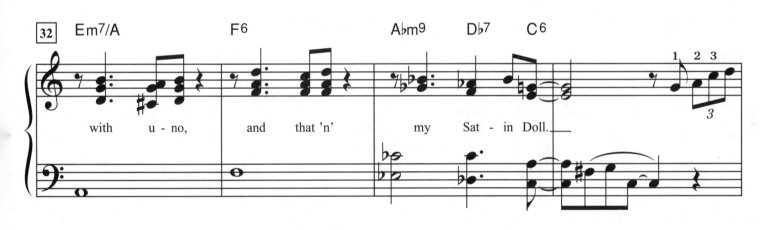

One of the most influential entertainment figures in the world, Charlie Chaplin was both a great comedian and a talented musician. For his 1936 movie *Modern Times,* which depicts his "Little Tramp" character attempting to cope with the industrialized age, he wrote the film, acted and composed the film score (with assists from Alfred Newman and David Raksin). Chaplin composed "Smile," the film's main theme, to which lyrics were later added. The song was recorded by many artists, most notably Nat King Cole.

SMILE

Music by Charles Chaplin
Words by John Turner and Geoffrey Parsons

Moderately, with great warmth

Smile, tho' your heart is ach - ing, smile, e - ven tho' it's break - ing, when there are clouds in the sky, you'll get by if you smile through your fear and sor - row, smile and may - be to - mor - row you'll see the sun come shin - ing through for you.

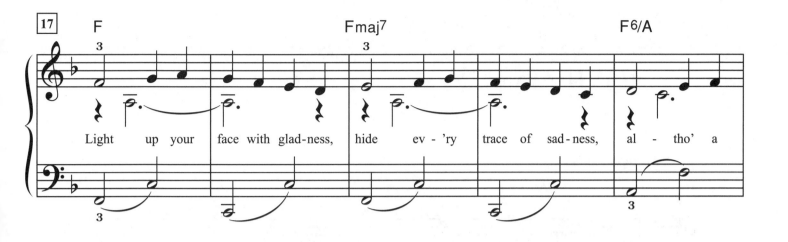

Light up your face with glad-ness, hide ev-'ry trace of sad-ness, al-tho' a

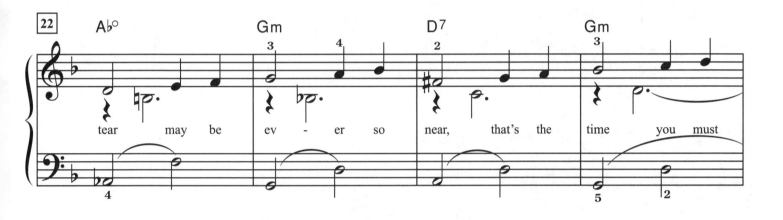

tear may be ev - er so near, that's the time you must

keep on try - ing, smile, what's the use of cry - ing? You'll find that

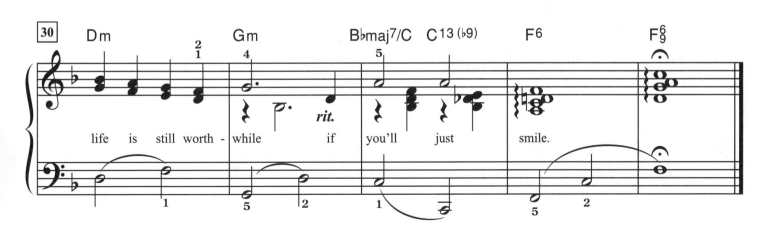

life is still worth - while if you'll just smile.

Originally composed as a vehicle for British musical-comedy star Gertrude Lawrence, "Someone to Watch over Me" appeared in the 1926 Broadway musical *Oh, Kay!* In the show, Miss Lawrence sang the song to a rag doll that she cuddled on stage.

SOMEONE TO WATCH OVER ME

Music and Lyrics by
George Gershwin and Ira Gershwin

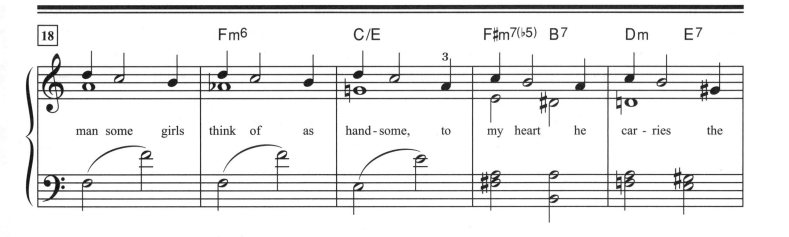

man some girls think of as hand-some, to my heart he car-ries the

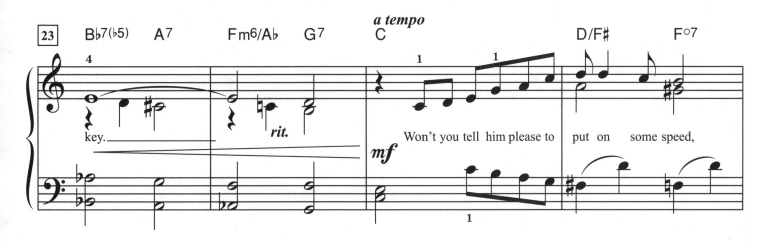

key. Won't you tell him please to put on some speed,

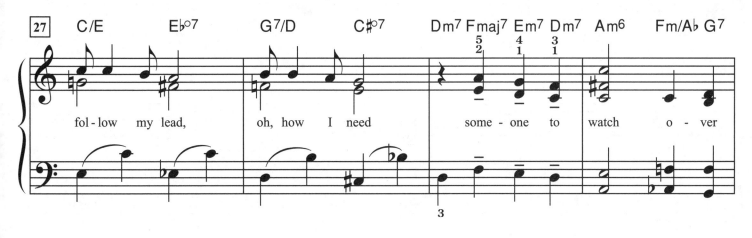

fol-low my lead, oh, how I need some-one to watch o- ver

me.

me.

French composer Maurice Jarre wrote this famous melody for the film classic *Doctor Zhivago*, based on Boris Pasternak's epic novel. The tune was initially dismissed by critics, but nevertheless became a popular standard that remains well loved to this day.

Somewhere My Love

Music by Maurice Jarre
Lyric by Paul Francis Webster

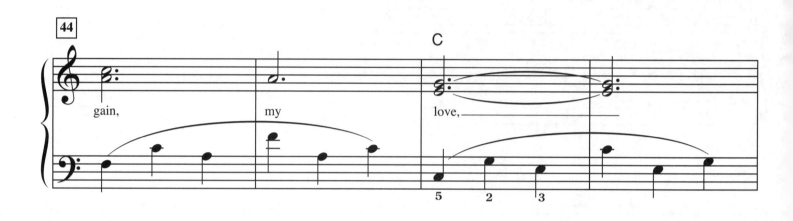

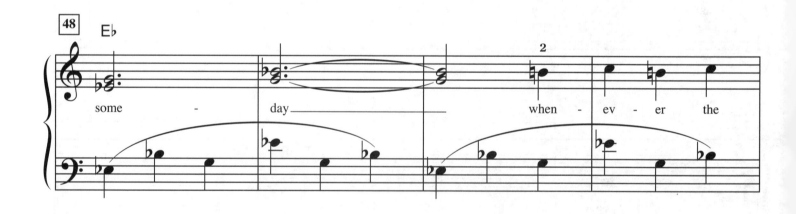

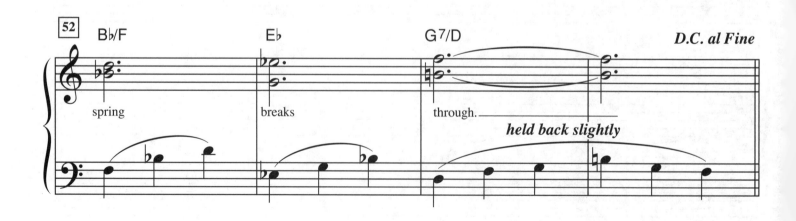

The original music and lyrics for this song were written by two German musicians. Later, Johnny Mercer supplied words in English, with music by Henry Mayer. Although Wayne Newton had the first hit with this song in 1965, it was Frank Sinatra's recording a year later that turned the song into an enduring standard.

SUMMER WIND

English Words by Johnny Mercer
Original German Lyrics By Hans Bradtke
Music by Henry Mayer

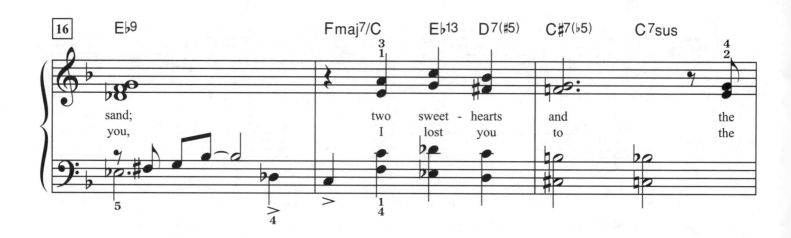

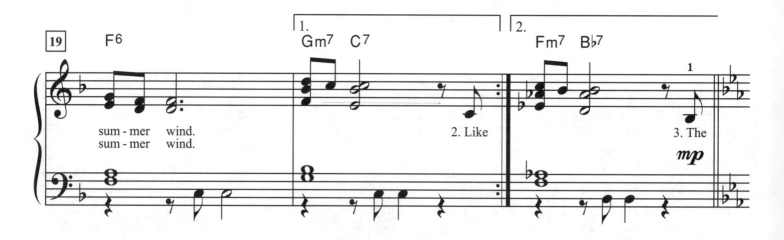

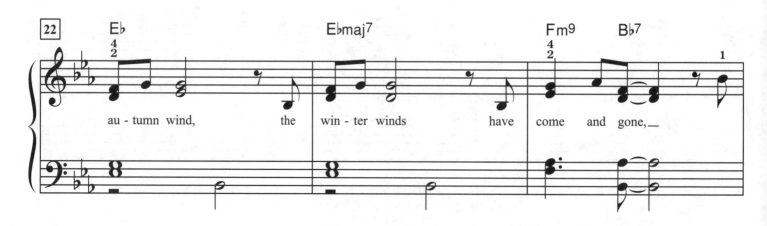

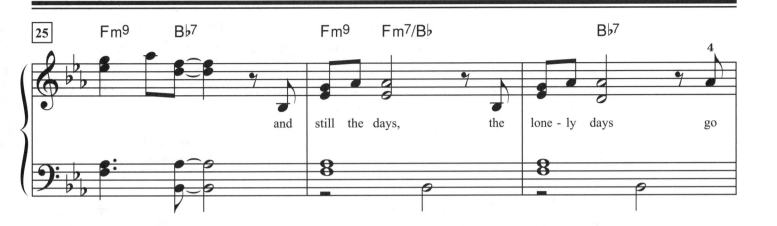

and still the days, the lone-ly days go

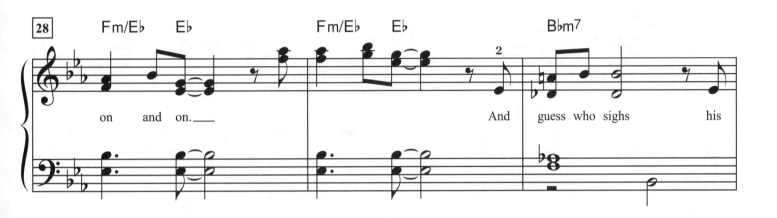

on and on.___ And guess who sighs his

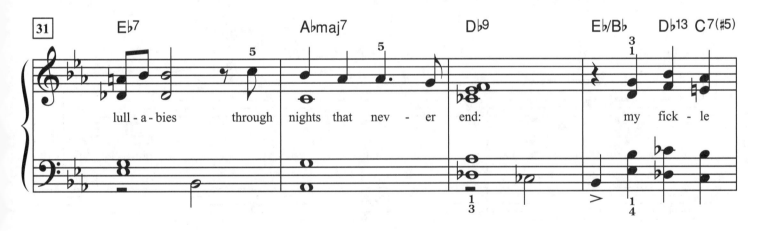

lull-a-bies through nights that nev-er end: my fick-le

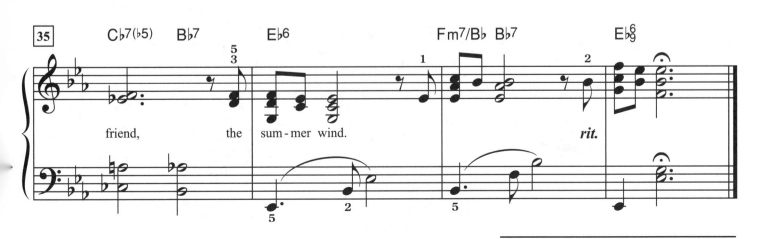

friend, the sum-mer wind. *rit.*

"Star Dust" remains one of the most-recorded songs of all time. Supposedly inspired by a Louis Armstrong trumpet solo, Hoagy Carmichael composed the melody in 1927, but it wasn't published until 1929. The introductory section is so lovely and well known that it is included in this arrangement.

STAR DUST

Music by Hoagy Carmichael
Words by Mitchell Parish

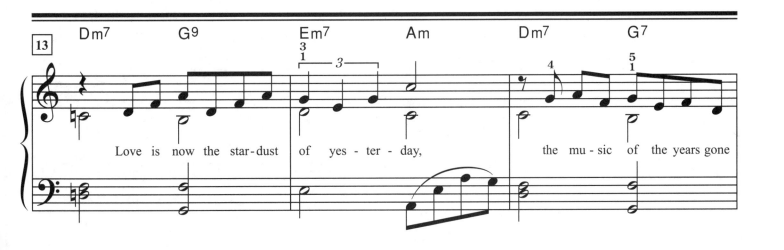

Love is now the star-dust of yes-ter-day, the mu-sic of the years gone

by. Some-times I won-der why I spend the lone-ly

night dream-ing of a song, the mel - o - dy

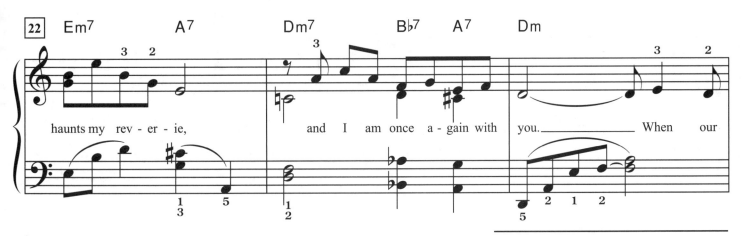

haunts my rev - er - ie, and I am once a-gain with you._____ When our

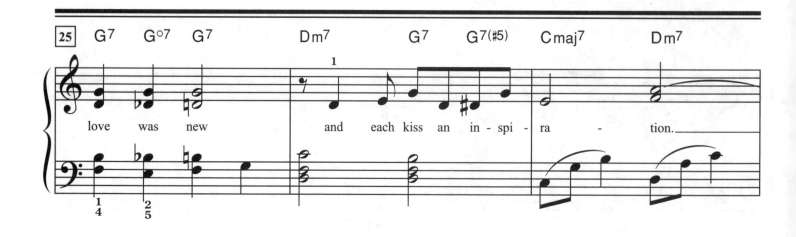

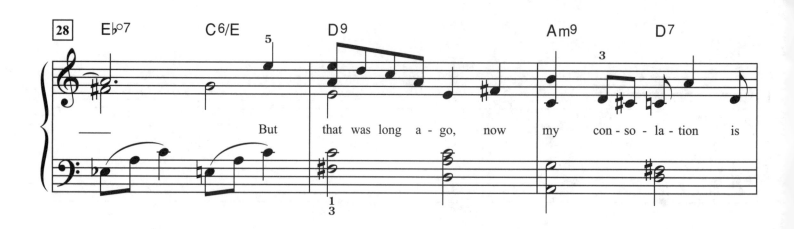

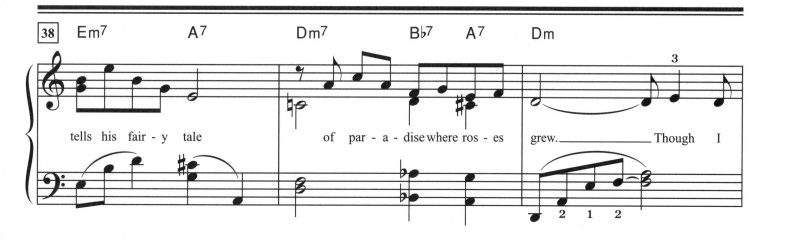

tells his fair - y tale   of par - a - dise where ros - es   grew.____ Though I

dream in vain,____   in my heart it will re - main: my

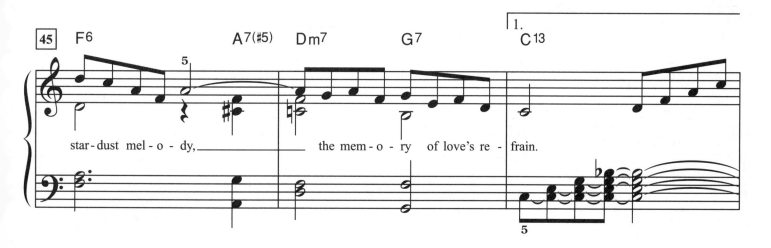

star-dust mel - o - dy,____   the mem - o - ry of love's re - frain.

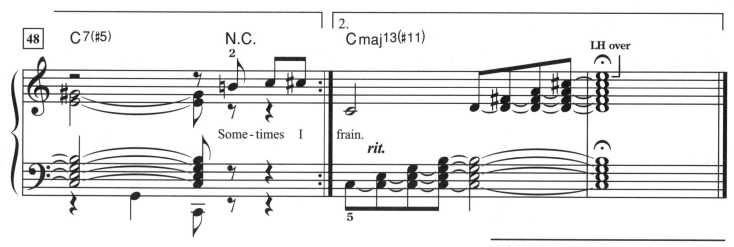

Some-times I | frain.

Billy Strayhorn wrote this jazz standard during the time he was associated with the great Duke Ellington and his band. The "A" train is a New York City subway line that runs up to Harlem. Sugar Hill, a posh neighborhood in Harlem, became a popular residential area among wealthy African-Americans during the Harlem Renaissance (1920s to early 1930s).

Take the "A" Train

Moderately fast swing

Words and Music by Billy Strayhorn

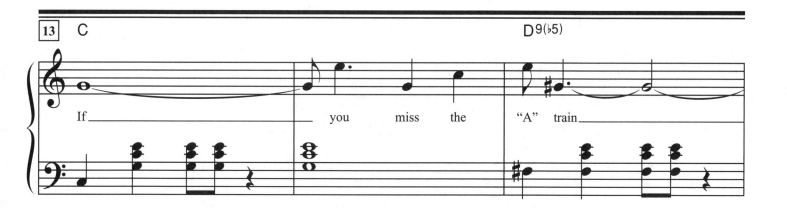

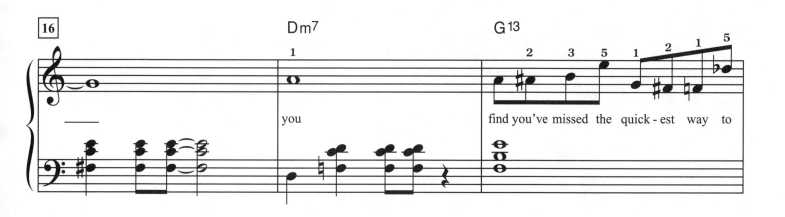

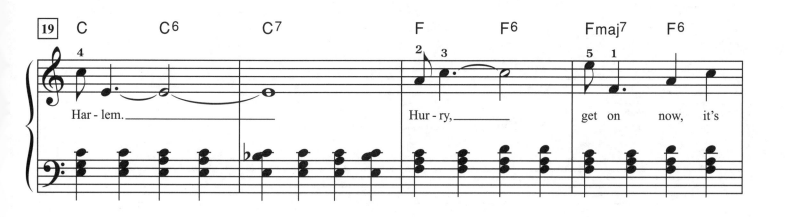

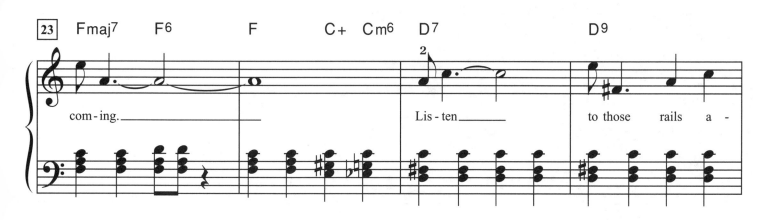

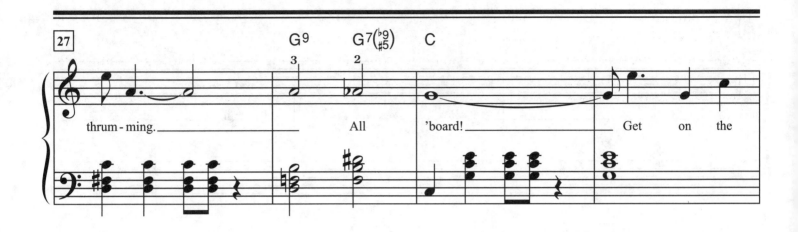

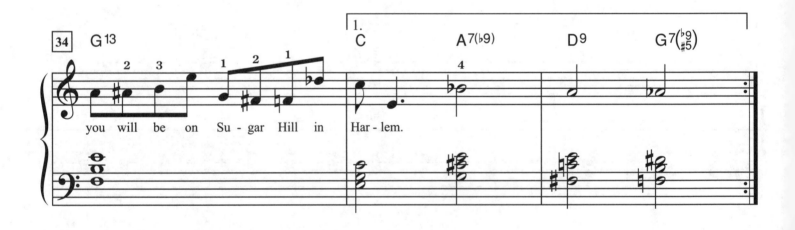

What a combination: Fred Astaire, Ginger Rogers, and George and Ira Gershwin. Written for the 1937 film *Shall We Dance*, this song is an example of a "laundry list" lyric, in which the writer gets an idea and comes up with many variations (for example, this song lists Christopher Columbus, Thomas Edison, Marconi, etc.).

THEY ALL LAUGHED

Music and Lyrics by
George Gershwin and Ira Gershwin

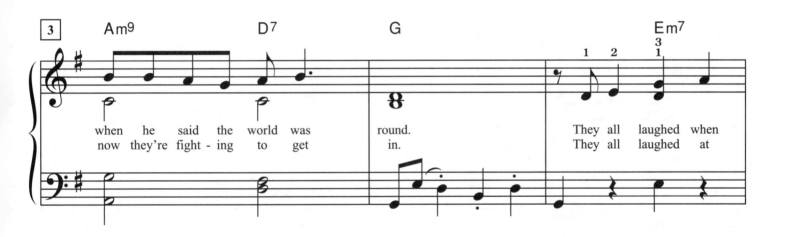

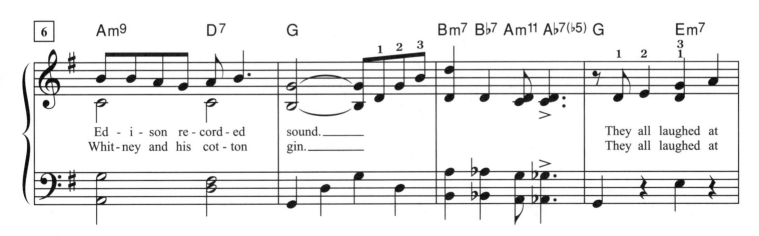

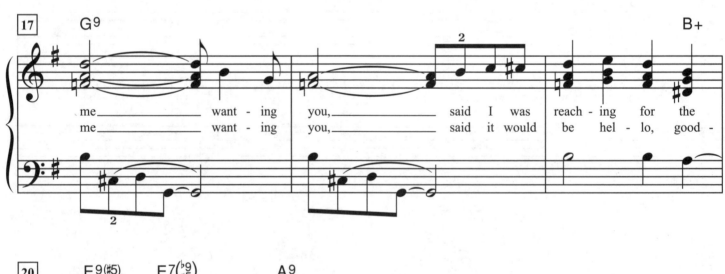

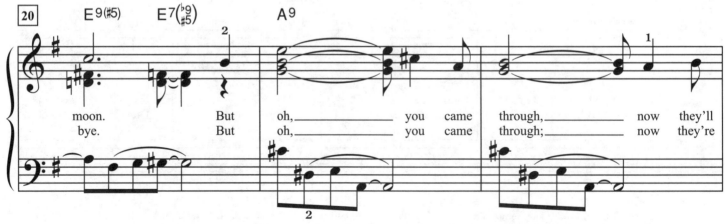

Yet another great Gershwin standard from the Fred Astaire/Ginger Rogers film *Shall We Dance*, this song immediately became a favorite among singers and jazz players. Tragically, George Gershwin died soon after the film came out. He was only 38 years old.

They Can't Take That Away from Me

Music and Lyrics by
George Gershwin and Ira Gershwin

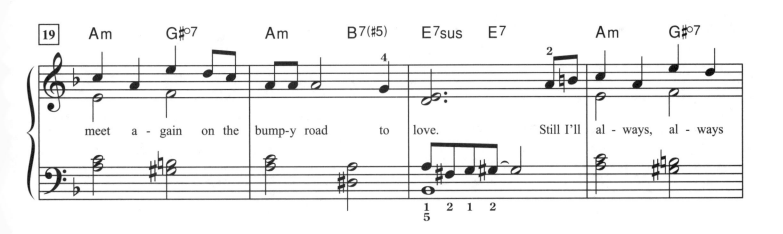

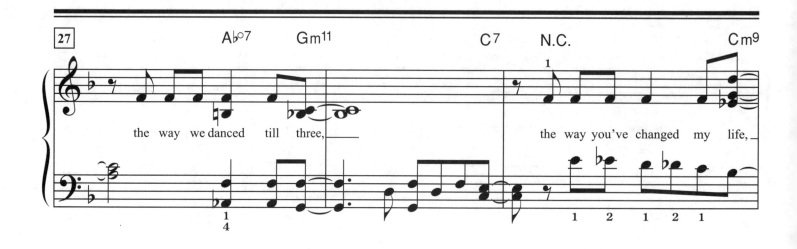

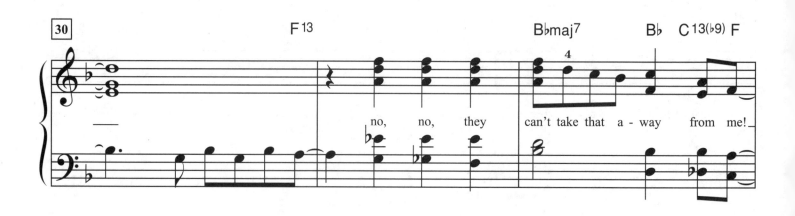

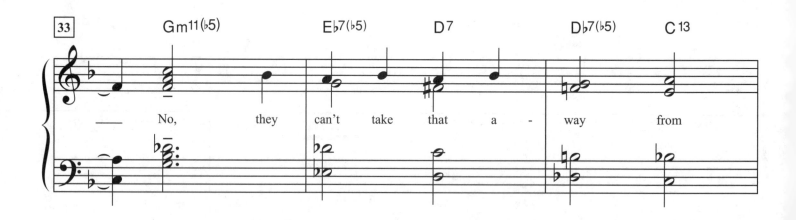

"Try a Little Tenderness" became a hit for Bing Crosby in 1933, and a couple of decades later Frank Sinatra made another outstanding recording of the piece. In 1966, this standard was given a soulful rendition by Otis Redding, and has remained a staple of the R & B circuit ever since.

TRY A LITTLE TENDERNESS

Words and Music by
Harry Woods, Jimmy Campbell and Reg Connelly

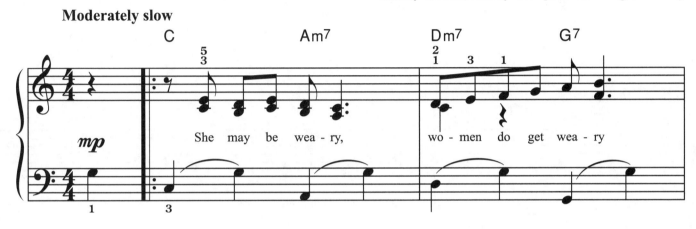

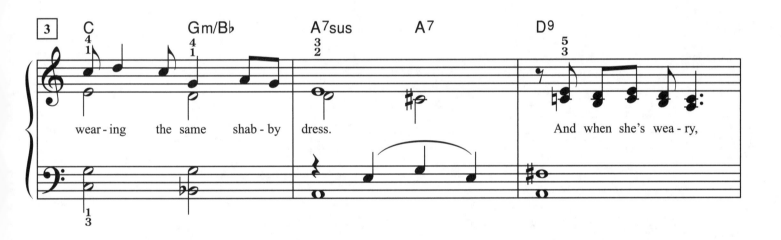

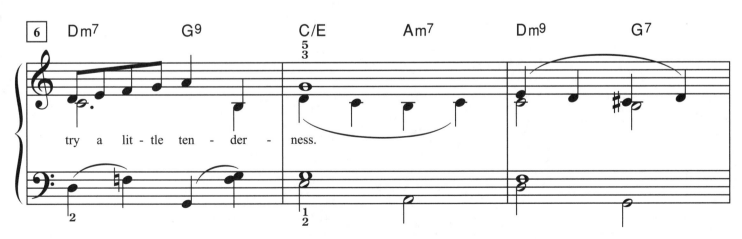

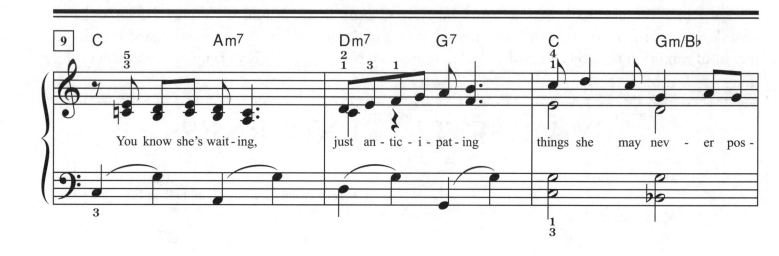

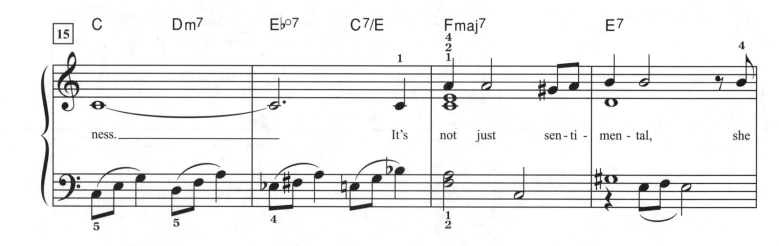

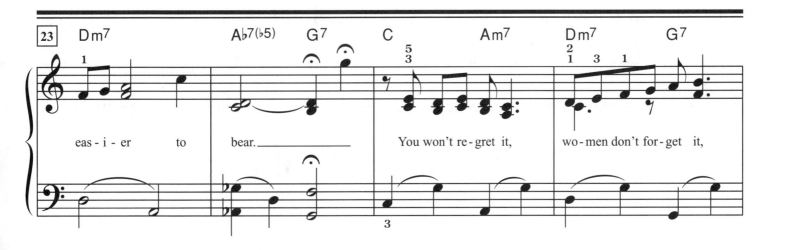

eas - i - er to bear._____ You won't re - gret it, wo - men don't for - get it,

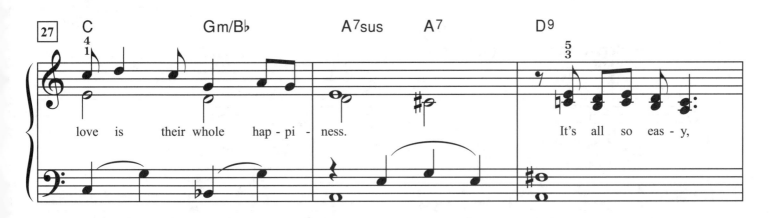

love is their whole hap - pi - ness. It's all so eas - y,

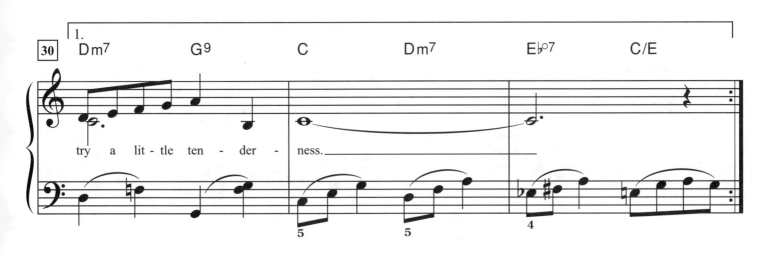

1.

try a lit - tle ten - der - ness._____

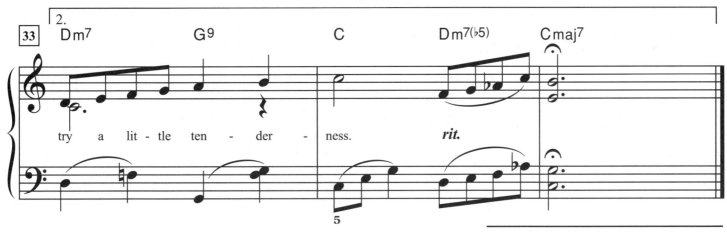

2.

try a lit - tle ten - der - ness. *rit.*

A huge 1951 hit by the "unforgettable" Nat "King" Cole, this song became a hit all over again by Natalie Cole, Nat's super-talented daughter. The magic of today's electronics allowed Natalie to sound as though she were singing a duet with Nat, long after he died—tragically young—of lung cancer in 1965.

UNFORGETTABLE

Words and Music by
Irving Gordon

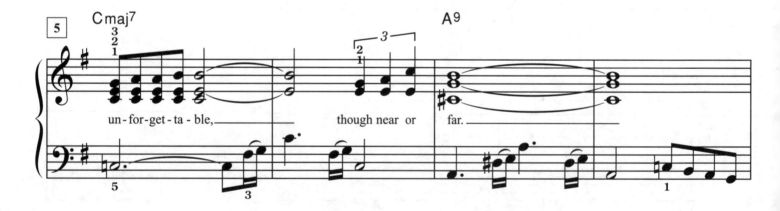

Sicilian singer/songwriter Domenico Modugno was unknown outside of Italy until he won the San Remo Song Festival by singing this tune under the title "Nel blu, dipinto di blu." It was such a big hit in Italy that Mitchell Parish added an English lyric, and under the title "Volarè" ("to fly"), Bobby Rydell's recording turned it into an American smash.

VOLARE

Music by Domenico Modugno
English Lyric by Mitchell Parish
Original Italian Text by Domenico Modugno
and Francesco Migliacci

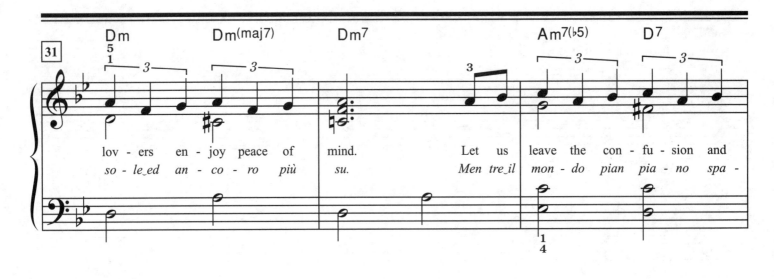

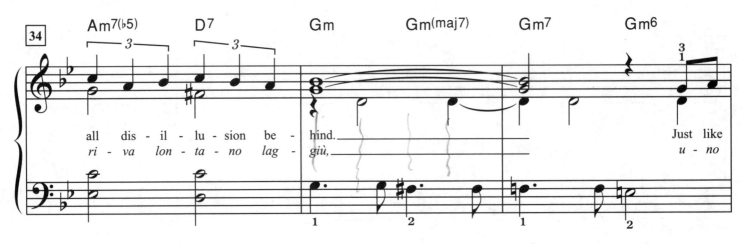

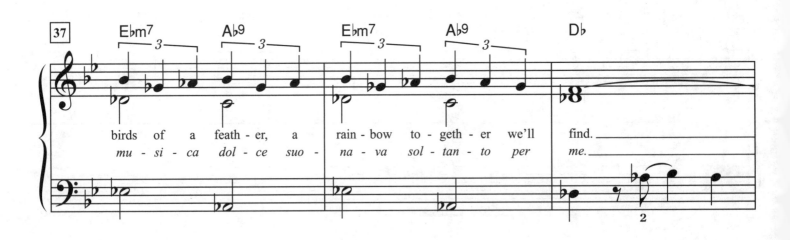

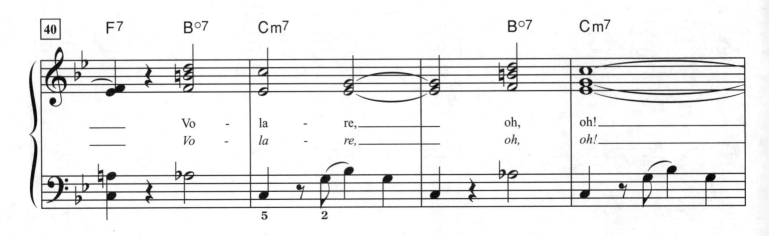

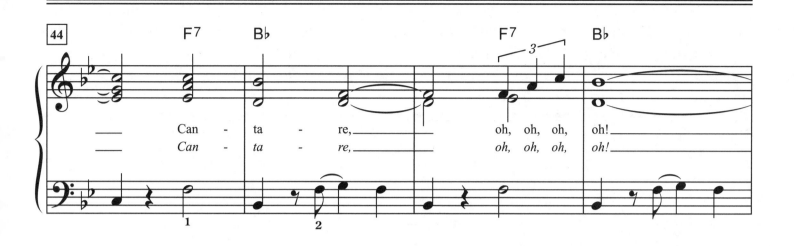

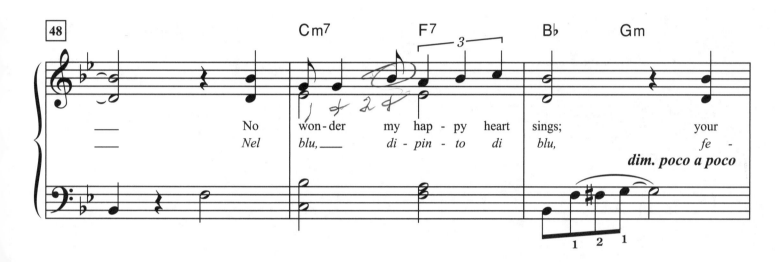

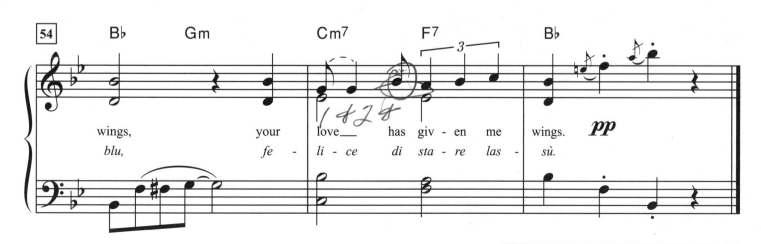

Beloved trumpeter/vocalist Louis "Satchmo" Armstrong was crucial to the development of jazz and swing. His trumpet playing influenced virtually every player of the period, and his inimitable vocal stylings echoed through the recordings of Bessie Smith, Billie Holiday, and many other singers. This 1967 song was Louis's last hit, and along with *Hello Dolly* is still his best-known work from an over 50-year career.

WHAT A WONDERFUL WORLD

Words and Music by
George David Weiss and Bob Thiele

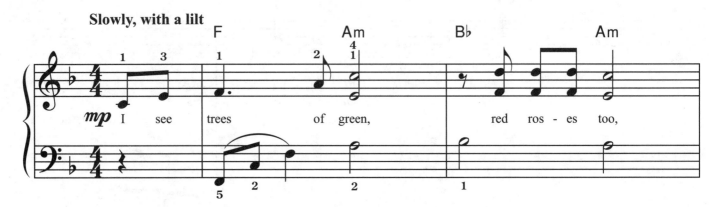

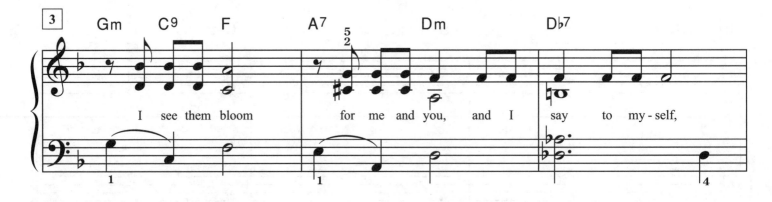

French composer Michel Legrand penned this hypnotic melody for the 1968 film *The Thomas Crown Affair*, starring Steve McQueen and Faye Dunaway. Actor Rex Harrison's son Noel performed the song for the film, but it is Dusty Springfield's version that is best known. Sting later covered the song, and his version was used in the 1999 remake of the film, starring Pierce Brosnan and Rene Russo.

THE WINDMILLS OF YOUR MIND

Words by Alan and Marilyn Bergman
Music by Michel Legrand

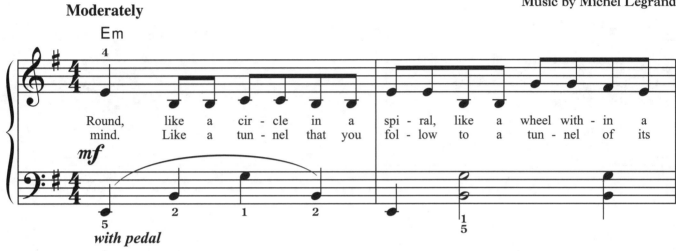

Round, like a cir - cle in a spi - ral, like a wheel with - in a
mind. Like a tun - nel that you fol - low to a tun - nel of its

wheel, nev - er end - ing or be - gin - ning on an ev - er spin - ning reel. Like a snow-ball down a
own, down a hol - low to a cav - ern where the sun has nev - er shone. Like a door that keeps re -

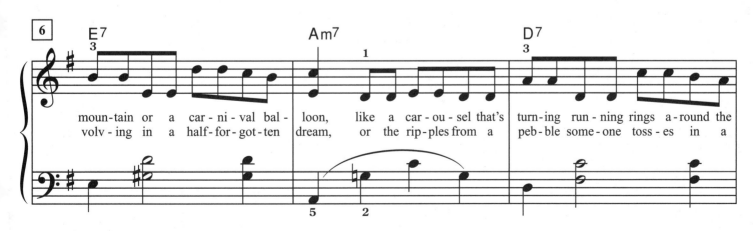

moun - tain or a car - ni - val bal - loon, like a car - ou - sel that's turn - ing run - ning rings a - round the
volv - ing in a half - for - got - ten dream, or the rip - ples from a peb - ble some - one toss - es in a

A number one single for "The Divine" Bette Midler, this lovely ballad was featured in the film *Beaches* (1988). Midler was not the first to record it, however. Gladys Knight had a minor hit with the song in 1982, and later it was recorded by Willie Nelson and others. Larry Henley has had hits both as a singer back in the 60s *(Bread and Butter)* and as a songwriter of Grammy-winners like this piece.

THE WIND BENEATH MY WINGS

Words and Music by
Larry Henley and Jeff Silbar

Although composed in 1946, it took 10 years until Frank Sinatra's swinging version of "You Make Me Feel So Young" turned this tune into a jazz standard. Other great singers who have also recorded this classic piece include Ella Fitzgerald, Mel Tormé and Rosemary Clooney.

You Make Me Feel So Young

Words by Mack Gordon
Music by Josef Myrow

¡Mira donde vivo!
Look Where I Live!

Un libro bilingüe busca y encuentra
A bilingual look-and-find book

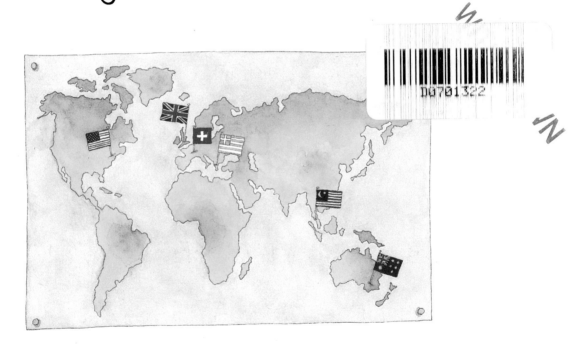

Lone Morton and Catherine Bruzzone
Illustrated by Louise Comfort
Language adviser: Rosa María Martín

b small publishing

Éste es Angus.
Vive en Escocia.
Angus tiene amigos en todo el mundo.

¿Quieres conocerlos?

This is Angus.
He lives in Scotland.
Angus has friends all around the world.

Would you like to meet them?

¡Aquí están!

Ahora pasa las páginas y descubre dónde viven.
Mira lo que puedes encontrar en el interior de sus casas.

Meilin

Sook Wing

Costas

Sam

Ross

Lily

Angus

Emilie   Pierre

Here they are!

Now turn the pages and discover where they live.
See what you can find inside their houses.

Costas y sus hermanos viven en Grecia.
Tienen seis gatos,
dos pares de botas de fútbol,
dos barcas de pesca pequeñas,
tres cestas de la compra,
cuatro alfombras,
un balón de fútbol,
seis platos bonitos y un baúl de madera.
Mira dentro de su casa. ¿Puedes encontrarlos?

Costas and his brothers live in Greece.
They have six cats,
two pairs of football boots,
two little fishing boats,
three shopping baskets,
four rugs,
one football,
six pretty plates and a wooden chest.
Look inside their house. Can you find them?

Lily vive en América.
Tiene tres televisores,
cuatro mochilas,
dos cuerdas de saltar,
un computador,
un telescopio,
cinco cojines,
tres plantas en macetas y una serpiente en un tanque.
Mira dentro de su casa. ¿Puedes encontrarlos?

Lily lives in America.
She has three televisions,
four rucksacks,
two skipping ropes,
one computer,
one telescope,
five cushions,
three plants in pots and a snake in a tank.
Look inside her house. Can you find them?

Ross vive en Australia.
Tiene dos tablas de surf,
tres raquetas de tenis,
tres toallas,
dos pelotas de playa,
dos pelotas de tenis,
un tren de juguete,
siete sombreros y un canguro de juguete.
Mira dentro de su casa. ¿Puedes encontrarlos?

Ross lives in Australia.
He has two surfboards,
three tennis rackets,
three towels,
two beach balls,
two tennis balls,
one toy train,
seven hats and a toy kangaroo.
Look inside his house. Can you find them?

Pierre y Emilie viven en Suiza.
Tienen un trineo,
cinco pares de zapatos,
dos pares de esquís,
una caja de chocolate,
un tambor,
tres fotos de la familia,
cuatro sillas de madera y un sillón azul y blanco.
Mira dentro de su casa. ¿Puedes encontrarlos?

Pierre and Emilie live in Switzerland.
They have one sledge,
five pairs of shoes,
two pairs of skis,
one box of chocolates,
one drum,
three family photographs,
four wooden chairs and one blue and white armchair.
Look inside their house. Can you find them?

Meilin y Sook Wing viven en Malasia.
Tienen dos máscaras de colores,
tres abanicos,
seis linternas chinas,
tres pares de zapatillas,
una máquina de coser,
dos dragones de papel,
cuatro cuencos azules y un pájaro amarillo en una jaula.
Mira dentro de su casa. ¿Puedes encontrarlos?

Meilin and Sook Wing live in Malaysia.
They have two colourful masks,
three fans,
six Chinese lanterns,
three pairs of slippers,
one sewing-machine,
two paper dragons,
four blue bowls and a yellow bird in a cage.
Look inside their house. Can you find them?

Sam vive en Inglaterra.
Tiene dos perros,
un soldado de juguete,
un par de botas,
dos ratones,
un caballo de balancín,
dos paraguas,
ocho cuadros y un cesto de manzanas verdes.
Mira dentro de su casa. ¿Puedes encontrarlos?
Angus hace una visita a Sam. ¿Puedes encontrar a Angus?

Sam lives in England.
He has two dogs,
one toy soldier,
one pair of boots,
two mice,
one rocking-horse,
two umbrellas,
eight pictures and a basket of green apples.
Look inside his house. Can you find them?

Angus is visiting Sam. Can you find Angus?

Mira las páginas anteriores y encuentra:
un bate de béisbol
dos plumas
tres bañeras
cuatro tablas de planchar
cinco telarañas
seis teléfonos
siete peces
ocho ositos
nueve relojes
diez espejos

(Las respuestas están marcadas con un círculo en las páginas 29-31.)

Look back through all the pages and find:
one baseball bat
two feathers
three baths
four ironing-boards
five spider's webs
six telephones
seven fish
eight teddy bears
nine clocks
ten mirrors

(The answers are ringed on pages 29-31.)

Las respuestas/Answers

La casa de Costas/Costas' house

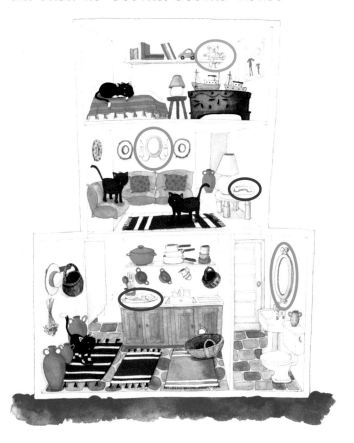

La casa de Lily/Lily's house

Las respuestas/Answers

La casa de Ross/Ross's house

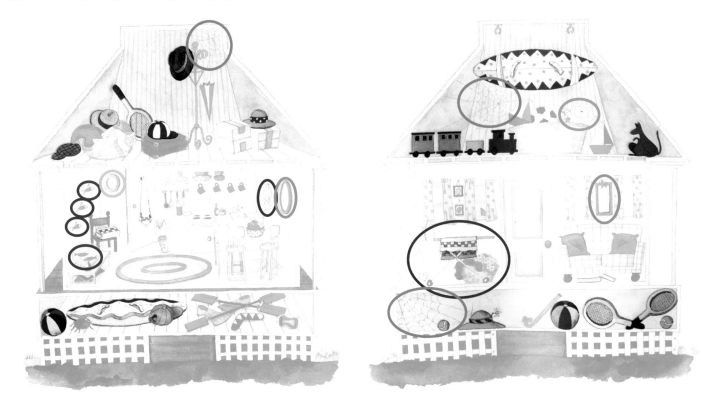

La casa de Pierre y Emilie/Pierre and Emilie's house

Las respuestas/Answers

La casa de Meilin y Sook Wing/Meilin and Sook Wing's house

La casa de Sam/Sam's house

Lista de palabras/Word List

Español-Inglés

el abanico fan
ahora now
la alfombra rug
amarillo/amarilla yellow
América America
el amigo/la amiga friend
aquí here
Australia Australia
azul blue
el balón de fútbol football
la bañera bath
la barca de pesca
  fishing boat
el bate de béisbol baseball bat
el baúl chest
blanco/blanca white
bonito/bonita pretty
la bota boot
la bota de fútbol football boot
el caballo de balancín
  rocking-horse
la caja box
el canguro kangaroo
la casa house
la cesta basket

la cesta de la compra
  shopping basket
chino/china Chinese
el chocolate chocolate
el cojín cushion
el computador computer
el cuadro picture
el cuenco bowl
la cuerda de saltar
  skipping rope
de madera wooden
dentro de inside
el dragón dragon
Escocia Scotland
el espejo mirror
el esquí ski
la familia family
la foto photograph
el gato cat
Grecia Greece
el hermano brother
Inglaterra England
la jaula cage
el juguete toy
la linterna lantern

la maceta pot
Malasia Malaysia
la manzana apple
la máquina de coser
  sewing-machine
la máscara mask
la mochila rucksack
el mundo world
el osito teddy bear
la página page
el pájaro bird
el papel paper
el par (de) pair (of)
el paraguas umbrella
la pelota ball
pequeño/pequeña little
el perro dog
el pez fish
la planta plant
el plato plate
la playa beach
la pluma feather
¿puedes...? can you...?
¿quieres...? would you like...?
la raqueta de tenis tennis racket

el ratón mouse
el reloj clock
la serpiente snake
la silla chair
el sillón armchair
el soldado soldier
el sombrero hat
Suiza Switzerland
la tabla de planchar
  ironing-board
la tabla de surf surfboard
el tambor drum
el tanque tank
la telaraña spider's web
el teléfono telephone
el telescopio telescope
el televisor television
el tenis tennis
la toalla towel
el tren train
el trineo sledge
verde green
y and
la zapatilla slipper
el zapato shoe

English-Spanish

America América
and y
apple la manzana
armchair el sillón
Australia Australia
ball la pelota
baseball bat el bate de béisbol
basket la cesta
bath la bañera
beach la playa
bird el pájaro
blue azul
boot la bota
bowl el cuenco
box la caja
brother el hermano
cage la jaula
can you...? ¿puedes...?
cat el gato
chair la silla
chest el baúl
Chinese chino/china
chocolate el chocolate
clock el reloj
computer el computador

cushion el cojín
dog el perro
dragon el dragón
drum el tambor
England Inglaterra
family la familia
fan el abanico
feather la pluma
fish el pez
fishing boat la barca de pesca
football el balón de fútbol
football boot la bota de fútbol
friend el amigo/la amiga
Greece Grecia
green verde
hat el sombrero
here aquí
house la casa
inside dentro de
ironing-board
  la tabla de planchar
kangaroo el canguro
lantern la linterna
little pequeño/pequeña
Malaysia Malasia

mask la máscara
mirror el espejo
mouse el ratón
now ahora
page la página
pair (of) el par (de)
paper el papel
photograph la foto
picture el cuadro
plant la planta
plate el plato
pot la maceta
pretty bonito/bonita
rocking-horse el caballo de balancín
rucksack la mochila
rug la alfombra
Scotland Escocia
sewing-machine
  la máquina de coser
shoe el zapato
shopping basket
  la cesta de la compra
ski el esquí
skipping rope
  la cuerda de saltar

sledge el trineo
slipper la zapatilla
snake la serpiente
soldier el soldado
spider's web la telaraña
surfboard la tabla de surf
Switzerland Suiza
tank el tanque
teddy bear el osito
telephone el teléfono
telescope el telescopio
television el televisor
tennis el tenis
tennis racket
  la raqueta de tenis
towel la toalla
toy el juguete
train el tren
umbrella el paraguas
web la telaraña
white blanco/blanca
wooden de madera
world el mundo
would you like...? ¿quieres...?
yellow amarillo/amarilla

32